IPH

PRO MAX CAMERA

USER GUIDE

The Complete Manual For Beginners & Seniors With Instructions On How To Master The iPhone 15 Pro Max Camera. With Photo Editing Tips & Tricks

By

Alan McDonald

Table of Contents

INTRODUCTION

They are the successors of the iPhone 14 and iPhone 14 Plus, and hence the seventeenth generation of iPhones overall. The more expensive iPhone 15 Pro and 15 Pro Max were unveiled at the same Apple Event on September 12, 2023 at Apple Park in Cupertino, California. The devices were made available for purchase on September 22, 2023, after a pre-order period that started on September 15.

History

The European Commission started deliberating in 2021 on a proposal to require USB-C on all devices sold in the European Union. According to Apple analyst Ming-Chi Kuo, Apple will no longer use the Lightning connection in its products by the year 2023. The possibility of the EU proposal passing at the time prompted Apple to explore switching to USB-C. In October of 2022, the proposal was signed into law as the Radio Equipment Directive. By the end of the month, Apple had affirmed that it would follow the rules.

It was stated two weeks before the official debut of the iPhone 15 that some of the devices will be offered throughout the globe for the first time on launch day.

An Exhibit of Hardware

The iPhone 15 has a 6.1-inch (155 mm), Super Retina XDR OLED display with a 60 Hz refresh rate, 2556 x 1179 resolution, and a pixel density of around 460 PPI. The 6.7-inch (170 mm) screen on the iPhone 15 Plus utilizes the same technology and refreshes at 60 frames per second; it has a resolution of 2796 by 1290 pixels and a pixel density of around 460 PPI. The Super Retina XDR OLED screen on both devices has increased brightness of up to 1,000 nits in normal use, 1,600 nits in HDR mode, and 2,000 nits in outdoor use. Instead of the display notch, the iPhone 15 has a new feature called Dynamic Island.[10] The iPhone 15 Pro and 15 Pro Max are the same dimensions as the iPhone 15 and iPhone 15 Plus, respectively.

Design

Both the standard iPhone 15 and the larger iPhone 15 Plus may be purchased in five distinct colors: black, blue, pink, yellow, and green. Since the iPhone XR, this is the first iPhone model to not debut with a (PRODUCT) RED option.

Name of the Colors

- ❖ Blue
- ❖ Pink
- ❖ Green
- ❖ Yellow
- ❖ Black

Rates of charging and data transmission

In contrast to the USB 3.2 Gen 2 transfer capabilities (estimated up to 10Gb/s or 1.25GB/s) of the iPhone 15 Pro and iPhone 15 Pro Max, the iPhone 15 and iPhone 15 Plus utilise USB-C at USB 2.0 transfer speeds (up to 480 Mb/s or 60MB/s)

Video Playback

All iPhone 15 models allow HDR video output at resolutions up to 4K through DisplayPort Alternate Mode via USB-C.

Due to technological limitations of the Lightning connection, the highest resolution that could be supported by older iPhone models (iPhone 5 through iPhone 14) using the Lightning Digital AV Adapter was 1600 x 900 (slightly less than 1080p).

Battery

Up to 26 hours of video playback and 100 hours of audio playback are available on the iPhone 15 Plus, while the iPhone 15 delivers up to 20 hours of video playback and 80 hours of audio playback, respectively.

Software

iOS 17 debuted with the new iPhone 15 models.Dynamic Island, a feature debuted with the iPhone 14 Pro series, will be included in all iPhone 15 models.

CHAPTER ONE

HOW TO QUICK LAUNCH YOUR IPHONE CAMERA

Give up the futile search for the Camera program!

To capture that priceless moment on your iPhone, you need to know how to quickly open the camera app. The majority of us now use our phones as cameras, making them constantly accessible; nevertheless, taking a picture is more complicated than just turning on the device and pressing the shutter button.

Thankfully, Apple realizes the significance of capturing this moment and has made it simple to quickly activate your iPhone camera. Learn the quickest methods to open the iPhone camera here!

The quickest way to access the iPhone camera(1)

Slide to the left to quickly access the iPhone camera.

Assuming you are beginning from the lock screen and not in the middle of using your phone, the quickest method to access the camera is to put your finger anywhere on the screen and then slide it all the way off to the left. As soon as you press it, the camera app will switch to photo mode, and you may start taking pictures in a matter of seconds.

The quickest way to access the iPhone camera(2)

A long press on the home button initiates the iPhone's camera.

The lock screen also supports using the power button instead of swiping to unlock the device. If you press and hold the camera symbol in the corner of the screen for half a second, the camera app will launch automatically. It's almost as fast and, depending on how you're holding your phone, could be easier.

Back Tap: The Fastest Way to Start Your iPhone's Camera

Here's a simple way to access the iPhone's camera: double-tap.

If you're prepared to navigate a few settings, you can configure your iPhone camera to activate when you double or triple press the back of the device. The first two choices are built into every iPhone.

Then, with two or three rapid touches to the rear of your phone, your camera will automatically open.

TAKE A PICTURE OR VIDEO

Find out the ins and outs of using your camera, from taking pictures to changing lenses.

Use the camera to take pictures, record videos, capture still images while recording, switch between the front and back cameras, focus, zoom in and out, see previously taken pictures, search for pictures, and more

How to Access Camera System

- Choose the Camera app from the main menu.
- Swipe left on the Lock screen to open the Camera app.
- Camera can be accessed from the Lock screen by tapping the thumbnail in the bottom left corner. From there, you can view and edit your photographs and videos.

Unlock your iPhone so you may send photographs and videos.

- Toggle between using the front and back cameras.

- Find the camera icon and click it. The Camera mode button.

While the video is being recorded, you cannot change the camera angle.

Acquire sharp focus

Simply tap the part of the image you want to zoom into. When you choose an area, a box will appear around

Focus in and out

Zoom in by dragging two fingers from the screen's center to the sides. To zoom out, drag two fingers inward from the screen's margins until the desired level of magnification is reached.

Click a picture.

- To begin recording, either click the Capture icon or use the volume controls.

To clarify, Live Photos is turned on by default. 1.5 seconds before and after a photograph is taken are captured in a live photo. You may turn off Live photographs by tapping the Live photographs icon in the Camera app. You may snap many shots quickly by holding down the Capture button or either volume button. As long as your finger is on the shutter button, the camera will keep snapping pictures. To get rid of an image, open the Photos app, find it, and then tap the trash can icon. To confirm, click the Delete Photo button. Check this out if you're experiencing issues with your iPhone's camera.

Make a recording

- Simply swipe right to access VIDEO and tap the record button to get started.
- You may stop a recording by pressing either volume button or by clicking the Stop symbol.
- Take a picture while recording a video.
- To start capturing images or video, tap the Capture button.

Look at hand-picked images

The Photos app will analyze your photo collection and recommend certain albums based on the finest photos you've taken that day, month, or year. Launch the Photos app from your home screen and tap the For You option.

Seek out pictures

Photos may be searched for using Spotlight's universal search. To access the search bar, swipe down from the home screen.

Put in the search term, then click on the picture you want.

To restrict your search to only the Photos app, choose Search in App.

Set iPhone's camera to manual mode

Find out how to take better pictures in less time, add special effects and filters, and see what's happening in the background of your shots by using the camera's more sophisticated functions.

Set the Primary Camera's Resolution

The default resolution for the main camera on iPhone 15 models is 24 megapixels. The resolution may be adjusted between 12 and 48 megapixels.

- Select between 12 MP or 24 MP under Settings > Camera > Formats > Photo Mode.
- Resolution Control or ProRAW & Resolution Control (depending on your model) may be used in the camera's settings to shoot at 48 megapixels.
- After activating ProRAW & Resolution Control on either the iPhone 15 Pro or iPhone 15 Pro Max, you'll be prompted to choose a default format through the Pro Default menu. Launch the camera app and use the format selector

toggle at the app's top. To change formats, touch and hold the toggle.
- Toggle the Outside View On/Off

On compatible devices, the camera preview will show you what's beyond the frame that can be captured by switching to a lens with a wider field of view. By default, "View Outside the Frame" will be enabled.

- View Outside the Frame may be disabled by selecting Settings > Camera > View Outside the Frame.

Prioritize Quicker Fire by Toggling It On and Off.

With Prioritize Faster Shooting enabled, photographs are processed differently, enabling you to take more shots in fast succession. Faster shooting is prioritized by default.

- Prioritize Faster Shooting may be disabled by selecting Settings > Camera > Prioritize Faster Shooting.

Flip the switch for lens correction.

Photos shot using the front or Ultra Wide camera on devices that support it might benefit from the Lens

Correction option. By default, lens correction will be on.

- Lens Correction may be disabled by selecting Settings > Camera > Lens Correction.

Scene Detection On/Off Switch

The Scene Detection feature on iPhone 12 models automatically determines what you're photographing and then applies an effect specifically designed to highlight relevant details. By default, scene detection will be enabled.

- Scene Detection may be disabled by selecting Settings > Camera > Scene Detection.

HOW TO LOCK FOCUS AND EXPOSURE SEPERATELY IN THE CAMERA APP ON IPHONE

Compatible iPhone cameras may now lock exposure independently of focus thanks to the exposure compensation function. You may lock the exposure and focus independently if you have trouble getting the right balance. This guide will walk you through the steps, explain which iPhones are supported, and highlight any caveats you should be aware of.

The mechanics of adjusting focus and light

In iOS 14, Apple finally included this function. If you're using an older version of iOS, you should read up on how locking focus and exposure works before moving on to the lesson proper.

Promotion and emphasis on iOS releases from the past

Prior to iOS 13, the Apple Camera app's focus and exposure controls were merged into a single slider. That's not great for iPhone photographers, and it's why some people turn to third-party applications like the critically acclaimed Halide Camera.

The iPhone's camera adjusts the focus and exposure before you press the shutter button, and up to 10 faces may be detected and averaged out before you take the picture. Here's how the prior emphasis and exposure adjustments worked:

- Simply tapping the screen will disclose the region of autofocus and the exposure value.
- Tap the screen in the new location to set the focus area's yellow square outline.

The exposure may be changed by dragging the vertical sun symbol up or down next to the focus area.

Manual focus and exposure settings may be locked for future photographs by tapping and holding the focus area until the "AE/AF Lock" (AE = Automatic Exposure; AF = Automatic Focus) icon appears. By doing so, you may avoid having these numbers update automatically whenever you move your iPhone's camera away from an object.

When shooting many photos of the same subject, locking focus and exposure may save a lot of time. Simply tapping the screen will reveal these secrets.

The iPhone's current focusing and lighting conditions

Locking manual exposure and focus is now possible on iOS 14 and later iPhones. This improves the Camera app's control and adds a touch of professionalism. The function is made available in the form of a novel exposure compensation variable (ECV). All images and videos shot during the current Camera session will be affected by the new value, and you may save the setting for future use.

Slide from Apple's press event showcasing the iPhone 11 Pro's improved camera quality, including the exposure focus compensation value

After AE/AF is locked, you may still easily adjust the brightness of your picture using the vertical sun slider. However, unlike previous iOS versions, touching anywhere in the camera viewfinder will no longer return your manual exposure adjustment to zero.

You may now lock the exposure value independently of the focus for an entire Camera session using the new ECV value, and you can still use the sun slider to fine-tune exposure for a single photo without affecting the ECV value for the whole session.

Electronics Compatibility Verification (ECV)

Only the iPhone XR, XS, and later models are compatible with the ECV function. This helpful photography function isn't available on handsets of a certain age.

Focus and exposure may be locked independently on iPhone cameras.

Focus and exposure may be locked independently in the iPhone's camera by following these steps:

- Launch the camera software.
- To access the toggle switches, swipe up or tap the chevron symbol.

- To use the new ECV knob, tap the "+/-" button.
- To adjust the shutter speed and f-stop from -2 to +2, use the horizontal ECV slider.

The iPhone camera's exposure button

To darken the picture, move the horizontal slider to the left, to around -2 degrees. In contrast, moving the slider to the right, towards +2, brightens everything. You may turn off the ECV adjustment by resetting the slider to its original position of zero.

Tap this option to show or conceal the ECV slider, and you'll even see a little live histogram change as you do so. Underexposed regions are represented by red bars on the left side of the histogram, while overexposed areas are represented by red bars on the right. If you're concerned about picture data loss due to extremes of brightness or darkness, this is a valuable tool.

As previously established, the vertical sun slider allows you to fine-tune exposure settings for a given photo beyond your current global ECV value, as seen in the GIFY animation below.

It is intended that the iPhone camera will continue to adjust exposure as you move the ECV slider. To avoid this, press and hold the appropriate region of the viewfinder until the "AE/AF Lock" icon appears, which will lock both the ECV and EV settings.

Camera session-spanning ECV preset saving

As previously indicated, the ECV slider stores your current exposure compensation setting for the duration of your Camera session, both for still images and movies. When you close the Camera app, the value will be reset to its default state. The ECV value and other camera settings may be saved automatically or manually on your iPhone. Here's what you need to do:

Get the iPhone's settings up and running.

- Select Camera from the main menu.
- Click the Save Changes button.
- Set the slide's exposure control to "ON."

Keep iPhone's Exposure Settings intact

iOS will now maintain your custom ECV setting across Camera sessions unless you modify it. That wraps up my comprehensive guide on the ECV function on the iPhone.

HOW TO TURN ON CAMERA FLASH ON IPHONE

Easy picture enhancement with the touch of a button.

Your continued support for How-To Geek is much appreciated. We may get compensation if you make a purchase after clicking on one of our affiliate links. Keep reading!

Connecting Dots

The iPhone's built-in flash may be easily activated in the Camera app if you're shooting a shot in low light and want to illuminate your subject. Different iPhone models have somewhat different procedures. Learn the steps here.

How To Enable Flash On Iphone With Face Id

The Camera app on an iPhone with Face ID (the iPhone X, 11, 12, or 13) looks a little different than it does on an iPhone with Touch ID (which we'll get to later). These gadgets have a convoluted set of steps for activating the flash.

- To begin, launch Camera and choose either the "Photo" or "Portrait" setting. If you're holding your iPhone vertically, the caret-

18

shaped arrow will be at the top-center of the screen; if you're holding it horizontally, it will be on the left.

- Select the arrow button on the left or top of the display.
- The menu that appears will be accessible from the side of the screen opposite the big white shutter button. Tap the lightning-bolt shaped flash symbol that appears in the new row of icons.
- Use the flash by clicking the symbol next to the shutter.
- Once you've tapped the lightning bolt symbol, a submenu will pop up underneath it with three choices: "Auto," "Flash On," and "Off." If you set your iPhone to "Auto," the flash will fire only when the Camera app detects low light. When the flash is "Flash On," it goes off every time the shutter is released. Do one of the following.
- When the flash is turned on, a flash icon (a yellow lightning bolt) will appear in a few different spots on the display.
- When Flash is turned on, the on-screen flash indicators will become bright yellow.

Simply reverse the steps above and choose "Off" from the flash menu. As an alternative, you may press the flash icon in the top-left (portrait) or bottom-left (horizontal) corner of the screen until the lightning bolt symbol is disabled.

Setting Up Flash on a Touch ID iPhone

The flash can be activated in two simple steps on any iPhone that has a home button and Touch ID (including the iPhone SE and all models prior to the iPhone 8). To take a photo in "Photo" or "Portrait" orientation, use the Camera app. The flash icon, shown as a lightning bolt, may be accessed by tapping the corresponding corner of the screen.

(Holding the phone on its side will place the flash icon in the bottom left corner. The symbol should be at the top left corner when held normally.

Select the flash symbol in the upper right.

A quick menu appears when the icon is tapped. Select "Auto" to have the flash fire automatically whenever the Camera app detects dim conditions. For consistent flash use in low-light situations, tap "On" to always use the flash.

- To access the submenu, choose

- A yellow lightning bolt icon will appear at the top of the screen whenever the flash is engaged. You may disable the flash by clicking the symbol once again and choosing "Off." I hope you enjoy yourself and get some fantastic shots.

USE IPHONE CAMERA TOOLS TO SET UP YOUR SHOT

You may utilize the Camera's editing features to get the perfect picture every time.

Focus and exposure may be adjusted.

The iPhone's camera automatically adjusts for focus and exposure before snapping a picture, and its face identification feature ensures that everyone in the shot is properly exposed. Focus and exposure may be changed by hand in the following ways:

Start recording.

- Select the region of autofocus and exposure by tapping the screen.
- The emphasis may be shifted by tapping the region of interest.
- To change the exposure, click the Adjust Exposure button next to the focus area and drag it up or down.

- Photography mode activated. The subject is brought into sharp focus in the viewfinder, and a brightness slider appears next to it.
- Tip: Touch and hold the focus area until you see AE/AF Lock to lock your manual focus and exposure settings for forthcoming photographs.
- The exposure for future photos may be precisely tuned and locked in on iPhone 11 and later. To change the exposure, open the camera's settings by tapping the gear icon, then hit the Exposure button. The exposure will remain set till you reopen Camera. Turn on Exposure Adjustment in Settings > Camera > Preserve Settings to prevent the exposure setting from being reset every time you open Camera.

Flip the switch for the flash.

The flash will activate automatically while taking photos with your iPhone. The following steps should be taken before to taking a shot in order to manually adjust the flash:

- You may toggle the auto-flash on and off by tapping the Flash button.

- Select Auto, On, or Off from the Camera Controls menu, and then hit the Flash button just below the viewfinder.

Filter your shot and snap it.

You may apply a filter to your picture to change the colors in it.

- Launch the camera and choose either the photo or portrait setting.
- Select Filters from the Camera Settings menu that appears.
- Using a swiping motion, you may quickly try out several filter effects before committing to one.
- To capture a picture with the selected filter, tap the Shutter button.
- The Photos app allows you to edit photos by adding or removing filters. For how to use filters, check out that section.

Start the clock.

In order to allow yourself enough time to get into the photo, you may use the timer function on your iPhone's camera.

- To access the camera controls, launch the camera app.
- Select between 3s or 10s by tapping the Timer button.
- To activate the timer, press the Shutter button.
- You can level your aim using a grid and a level.
- Select Settings > Camera > Grid and Level to show a grid or level on the camera screen, which may be used to align and arrange your shots.

The Photos app's editing capabilities allow you to fine-tune horizontal and vertical perspective after you've taken a picture.

Learn how to automate your photo editing on your iPhone by using Photographic Styles.

Using the iPhone's Photographic Styles, you can easily and automatically make your photos seem professional.

It's not uncommon for photographers to feel the complete opposite of the way I do about the prospect of spending many hours in front of the greatest photo editing software. Even if you know how to edit images on an iPhone, it's fair to feel that it isn't worth the effort considering how frequently iPhones and smartphones are used only for casual shots.

But what if you never had to manually edit a picture again since it would be automatically edited as you took it? Photography "looks" are where they come in handy. This little-known feature of the iPhone camera lets you apply effects to your shots in real time. It may enhance the contrast, color, warmth, or coldness of your photographs. Leave your phone alone after configuring a Photographic Style to have that appearance applied to all future photos.

Be aware that after you've edited a picture using Photographic Styles on your iPhone, you can't go back and change anything about it.

Also, please take notice that this function is currently only compatible with the iPhone 13, iPhone 14, and the iPhone SE (3rd Gen). You may wish to learn how to make changes by copying and pasting on iPhone instead if you have an earlier model. With the copy/paste changes feature in iOS Photos, you can use the Photographic Styles app to apply the same set of adjustments to a number of photographs with a single tap. It's not quite as automated as Photographic Styles, but it's still quite

25

simple and may be used to swiftly apply the same effects to several pictures.

Setting iPhone Camera Effects

- When in Photo mode, open the Camera app and slide up to see the three squares.
- Use your finger to swipe left to see different photographic effects.
- when you find a Photography Style you like, hit the sliders to enlarge them, and then use the newfound control to adjust the Photography Style's overall tone and warmth.
- Take a picture using the Photographic Style while you're feeling cheerful.
- The Settings menu is where you'll discover Photographic Styles and all the information you need about them. This technique allows you to choose a Photographic Style and provides a short explanation of their impact. In the Settings app's Camera section, choose Photographic Styles.
- To view the effects of each style on a picture, just swipe through them; when you find one you like, hit Use "Style" to apply it.
- You don't need to add Photographic Styles as a preserved camera option; once selected, your camera will utilize that Style until you change

it back to Standard. These Styles are baked into the picture, so to speak; you cannot erase or eliminate their impact, giving you less freedom in post-production, so remember to switch the camera back to Standard if you want to edit the photographs later.

CHANGE ADVANCED CAMERA SETTINGS ON IPHONE

Find out how to use the camera's more complex settings to take pictures faster, add special effects and filters, and see things that are normally hidden from view.

Modify the Resolution of the Primary Camera

The default resolution for the main camera on iPhone 15 models is 24 megapixels. The resolution may be changed from 12 MP to 24 MP to 48 MP.

- Select between 12 MP or 24 MP under Settings > Camera > Formats > Photo Mode.
- Resolution Control or ProRAW & Resolution Control (depending on your model) may be used in the camera's settings to shoot at 48 megapixels.
- Select Pro Default after activating ProRAW & Resolution Control on your iPhone 15 Pro or

iPhone 15 Pro Max, and then select your preferred default format. Toggle the format you want to use on and off by opening Camera and tapping the corresponding toggle at the top of the screen. To change formats, touch and hold the toggle.

- If you own an iPhone 15 Pro or iPhone 15 Pro Max, you may alter the main camera lens to suit your needs by visiting Customize the main camera lens.
- Toggle the Outside View On/Off
- On compatible devices, the camera preview will show you what's beyond the frame if you have a wider-angle lens installed in the camera system. By default, "View Outside the Frame" will be on.
- View Outside the Frame may be disabled by selecting Settings > Camera > View Outside the Frame.

Flip the switch to prioritize rapid fire.

When you touch the Shutter button fast, the Prioritize Faster Shooting option adjusts the picture processing so that you can take more shots. Faster shooting is prioritized by default.

- Select Settings > Camera > Prioritize Faster Shooting to disable the feature.

Lens Correction may be toggled on and off.

When enabled, the Lens Correction option improves the appearance of selfies and ultra wide shots produced with compatible devices. By default, lens correction will be on.

- You may disable Lens Correction by going to Settings > Camera > Lens Correction.

Activate and deactivate scene detection

The Scene Detection feature on iPhone 12 models automatically determines what you're photographing and then applies an effect specifically designed to highlight relevant details. By default, Scene Detection will be activated.

- Settings > Camera > Scene Detection Off will disable Scene Detection.

CHAPTER TWO

EDIT LIVE PHOTOS ON IPHONE

Live Photos may be edited in the Photos app using effects like Bounce and Loop, and the main photo can be swapped out.

Real-Time Image Manipulation

You can edit a Live Photo just like any other photo on your iPhone, swapping out the primary image, shortening the clip, turning off the audio, and even saving it as a still image.

The Live Photo itself is the focal point of this screen. The picture viewer has a Make Key Photo button that's currently enabled underneath the image. The Live Photo may be cropped using the two arrows located on each end of the frame viewer. The Live, Adjust, Filters, and Crop controls are located at the bottom of the display. There is a click on the Live button. The Cancel button is located in the top left corner, while the Done button may be found on the top right. The screen's top row of buttons also includes options to mute the audio, go live, add annotations, and activate other plugins.

- Launch the iPhone's photo album.

- Select Edit after opening a Live Photo.

You may do any of the following after tapping Live Photo:

- To choose a primary image, slide the white frame in the viewer, select Make Key Photo, and finally select Done.
- A Live Photo may be trimmed by selecting which frames to play by dragging the frame viewer's left or right edges.
- Create a still image by: To disable Live, tap the Live button in the screen's upper-right corner. The main shot from a Live shot is captured as a still image.
- When viewing a Live Photo, tap the top-right "Mute" button to silence it. Repeatedly tapping the screen will turn off the mute.

Changing the key picture in a Live picture produced with an iPhone 15 will nullify the portrait effect.

Change the look of a Live Photo.

Live Photos may be edited into entertaining short films by applying various filters.

- Launch the iPhone's photo album.
- Throw open a Live Pic.

- Select one of the following options when you tap Live in the upper left corner of your screen:
- ➤ Live: Utilizes the real-time video streaming capability.
- A looped video plays the same scene over and over again.
- To "bounce" is to reverse and then resume play.
- ➤ Long Exposure: Creates motion blur to resemble that achieved by a DSLR set to a long exposure.
- Live Off deactivates the Live video feed and any effects it may have applied.

TAKE PORTRAITS WITH YOUR IPHONE CAMERA

When shooting with the camera app in Portrait mode, your subject (people, pets, objects, and more) will remain in fine focus while the foreground and backdrop are artistically softened. The lighting in your photographs may also be changed and customized.

Use the Portrait setting to snap a photo.

Viewfinder of camera set to "Portrait" mode, where the subject is in focus but the surrounding is blurred. Studio Light is now chosen on the portrait lighting dial at the bottom of the frame. The Flash button may be found in the upper left corner, the Camera Controls button in the middle, and the Portrait Lighting intensity and Depth Control buttons in the upper right corner. The Camera Chooser Back-Facing button, the Take Picture button, and the Photo and Video Viewer button may all be found at the screen's base, from left to right.

- Launch the camera app and go to Portrait mode.
- Frame your subject in the yellow portrait box according to the on-screen instructions if requested to do so.
- Zoom in or out by tapping the 1x, 2x, or 3x buttons on compatible devices.
- Pinch the screen to zoom in and out on iPhone 15 models.

You may adjust the lighting by dragging the Portrait Lighting slider.

- ➢ Exposure to natural light; subject is in focus while the surrounding is out of focus.
- ➢ Studio lighting: the subject's face is well illuminated, and the image is crisp and clear.

Highlights and lowlights provide dramatic shading on the face under contour lighting.

Spotlights on the face illuminate the stage, which is otherwise dark.

It's a lot like the Stage Light effect, but in timeless black and white.

The high-key light monochrome setting makes the foreground gray and the backdrop white.

To snap a picture, just press the shutter button.

If you snap a picture in Portrait mode and then decide you don't like the portrait effect, you may easily delete it. To enable or disable the effect, open the picture in the Photos app, choose Edit, and finally Portrait.

Take note that while using the wide (1x) lens for a portrait in low light, Night mode will automatically activate on models that are compatible with it.

Keep in mind that Portrait mode photographs may be modified using Photography Styles.

Note that the Stage Light, Stage Light Mono, and High-Key Light Mono modes are exclusive to the front-facing camera on the iPhone XR.

Tweak Portrait Mode's Depth Control

- To modify the blurring effect of the backdrop in your portraits, use the Depth Control slider.
- To take a portrait, open the camera app and switch to the portrait mode.
- Select the Depth Adjustment menu from the menu bar.

A frame-level Depth Control slider is provided.

The effect may be modified by dragging the slider to the right or left.

To snap a picture, just press the shutter button.

After taking a photograph, you can tweak the level of background blur using the Depth Control slider in the Photos app. See also Portrait Mode Editing.

Modify the Portrait Mode's Lighting

You may realistically tweak the location and strength of the Portrait Lighting to highlight eyes or soften creases in the skin.

- To pick a lighting effect, open Camera, switch to Portrait mode, and then use the slider on the Portrait Lighting control.
- Select Portrait Control from the menu bar.

The Portrait Lighting control bar is located just below the picture.

The effect may be modified by dragging the slider to the right or left.

To snap a picture, just press the shutter button.

Portrait Lighting may be adjusted in the Photos app after a photo has been taken. See also Portrait Mode Editing.

Do a self-portrait using the camera's Photo setting.

Photos shot in Photo mode on iPhone 15 models may have the backdrop blurred for a portrait look.

Camera display when set to "Photo" mode, where subjects stand out against a blurred backdrop. The Depth button (located in the viewfinder's lower-left corner) is pressed in order to achieve the portrait mode.

Cameras wide open!

When your iPhone's camera identifies an object, such as a human, dog, or cat, the Depth button will appear at the viewfinder's bottom.

When the Depth button appears in Photo mode, your iPhone will record depth information that may be used to create a portrait effect after the fact in the Photos app. Tapping a subject in the viewfinder to concentrate on it will trigger the appearance of the Depth button. Tapping a different topic in the viewfinder will shift the portrait's focus to that area.

First, choose the desired depth of field by tapping the Depth button, and then capture the picture by using the Shutter button.

In the Photo mode, you may apply a Photographic Style to the portrait.

CAPTION ACTION SHOTS WITH BURST MODE ON YOUR IPHONE CAMERA

Camera's Burst mode is useful for snapping many quick shots of a moving subject or for getting a variety of shots at once. Both the back and the front-facing cameras support Burst mode.

- Launch the iPhone's camera app.
- For a leftward swipe, use the shutter button.
- Raise a finger to indicate a halt.
- press the Burst thumbnail, and then press Select, to choose which shots to save.

The thumbnails with the gray dot under them are the ones we recommend you save.

If you wish to save each picture separately, hit the circle in the photo's lower-right corner, and then tap Done.

- By tapping the thumbnail and then the Delete button, the whole Burst may be removed.

TAKE A SELFIE WITH YOUR IPHONE CAMERA

Make a self-portrait using the camera. Selfies may be captured in either still image or moving picture format.

Altering the camera's shooting mode may be found at that link.

- Launch the iPhone's camera app.
- To use the front-facing camera, choose it from the Camera Chooser by tapping the Front-Facing button.

Keep your iPhone in plain view.

- To expand your field of vision, try tapping the arrows within the frame.
- To begin recording or snapping photos, use the volume controls.

The Photo & Video Viewer, Take Picture, and Camera Chooser Back-Facing buttons may be found to the right of the camera mode menu. At the very top of the display, you'll find shortcuts to Flash, Camera Settings, and Live Photos. They're all snapping selfies inside the frame.

- By selecting Settings > Camera > Mirror Front Camera, you may shoot a selfie that records the scene as you view it from the front-facing camera, rather than in reverse.

TAKE PANORAMIC PHOTOS WITH YOUR IPHONE CAMERA

To capture the whole environment in one shot, switch your Camera to Pano mode.

Altering the camera's shooting mode may be found at that link.

- Launch the iPhone's camera app.
- Flip to Pano.
- Simply press the shutter button.
- Slowly follow the arrow, making sure it stays in the middle of the screen.
- To conclude, press the Shutter button one again.

- To move the camera in the other way, tap the arrow. Turn your iPhone to landscape mode to scroll vertically. An inverted vertical pan is also possible.

TAKE MACRO PHOTOS AND VIDEOS WITH YOUR IPHONE CAMERA

In order to take outstanding macro photographs, Camera makes advantage of the Ultra Wide camera on compatible devices. Macro, Live, slow-motion, and time-lapse photography and videography are all possible.

Capture a close-up image or recording of anything

- Launch Camera on your iPhone and choose between taking photos and recording videos.
- Come within 2 cm of your topic. Switching to Ultra Wide mode will occur automatically.
- Use the record and shutter buttons to begin and end video recording.

Create a time-lapse or slow-motion macro video.

To take a time-lapse or slow-motion photo with your iPhone, use the Camera app.

- Select the Ultra Wide angle by pressing the.5x button and getting very close to your subject.
- You may begin and end recordings by tapping the Record button.

Manage the transitioning of automated macros

The Ultra Wide setting may be set to go on automatically while taking macro shots or films.

- Launch the iPhone's camera app and get in close to your subject.
- When you are sufficiently enough to your subject, the Auto Macro On button will activate automatically.
- To disable the automatic switching of macros, tap the Auto Macro On button.
- If the image or video gets fuzzy, try pressing back or tapping again.Multiply it by 5 to activate the Ultra Wide lens.
- To enable automatic macro switching again, tap the button labeled "Auto Macro Off."
- Disabling Macro Control in Settings > Camera prevents the device from automatically switching to the Ultra Wide camera while taking macro shots.

- The Macro Control option may be preserved across sessions by activating Settings > Camera > Preserve Settings.

HOW TO DISABLE NIGHT MODE ON YOUR IPHONE'S CAMERA

When the iPhone's camera detects a dark situation, either inside or out, the Night Mode setting activates automatically, resulting in more accurate colors and less noise. That's the plan, at least. The truth is that you can't always rely on Night Mode to get the perfect evening shot.

Activate/ deactivate Night mode

To avoid overexposed photos caused by Night Mode, switch it off when you want to capture a true nighttime scene in which all sources of light are muted.

When shooting in dim conditions, Night Mode will automatically be activated until you disable it by touching the yellow Night Mode button that displays at the top of the viewfinder. The issue is that if you reopen the Camera app and the sensor detects low light, Night Mode will activate once again.

There was no permanent option to turn off Night Mode in iOS 14; you had to manually deactivate it each time you opened the Camera app. However, on iOS 15 and later, you may disable Night Mode and have it persist across successive Camera app launches. The steps are as follows.

- Open the iPhone's Settings menu.
- Connect Camera.
- Select "Keep Preferences" to save your changes.
- Set the Night Mode switch to the "ON" position, which is the green button.

When you turn off Night Mode, the camera will remember that setting for the next time you use it. You can still activate Night Mode in the Camera app in the traditional manner, but you'll have more say over when it kicks in.

TAKE APPLE PRORAW PHOTOS WITH YOUR IPHONE CAMERA

Camera allows you to capture images in Apple ProRAW on compatible devices. Apple ProRAW combines the data from a regular RAW format with the processing power of the iPhone to give you more leeway in terms of artistic expression when adjusting things like exposure, color, and white balance.

All cameras, including the front-facing one, support Apple ProRAW. Portrait orientation does not work with Apple ProRAW.

Implement Apple's ProRAW

On models that are compatible with Apple ProRAW, you may enable it by going to Settings > Camera > Formats and toggling on Apple ProRAW or ProRAW & Resolution Control.

Apple ProRAW photographs are bigger because they save more data about the photographed subject.

To use Apple ProRAW, open the camera app, take a picture, and then either hit the Raw Off button or the Raw 12 Switch Button Off button, depending on your device.

You can toggle ProRAW on and off while shooting by pressing either the Raw On or Raw Off button, or the Raw 12 Switch Button On or Raw 12 Switch Button Off.

- Turn on Apple ProRAW or ProRAW & Resolution Control and save your camera's settings by selecting Settings > Camera > Preserve Settings.

Modify the resolution and file type of Apple's ProRAW by default

You may alter the default ProRAW resolution to either 12 MP, 48 MP, or HEIF 48 MP on the iPhone 15 Pro, iPhone 15 Pro Max, iPhone 14, and iPhone 14 Max.

- Select "Camera" > "Formats" > "Settings"
- ProRAW and Resolution Control should be activated.
- Select the default resolution and file type by tapping the Pro Default button and then selecting either HEIF Max, ProRAW 12 MP, or ProRAW Max.

Take note that if you've set your camera to "Most Compatible," then JPEG Max will be utilized instead of HEIF Max.

CHAPTER THREE

RECORD VIDEOS WITH YOUR IPHONE 15 CAMERA

The iPhone's Camera app may be used to create both regular video and QuickTake videos. Master switching shooting modes to capture slow-motion or time-lapse footage.

Make a recording

- Release the shutter and switch to video.
- To begin recording, push either volume button or tap the Record button. The following are options when recording:
- To snap a still image, just tap the white Shutter button.
- To zoom in or out, just pinch the screen.
- To zoom in even more (on compatible devices), press and hold the 1x icon, and then use your finger to move the slider.
- To stop recording, tap the Record button or use the volume controls.

Please take note that a green dot will show at the top of the screen to indicate that the camera is active for your safety.

Capture high-definition or ultra-high-definition video.

High-definition (HD), ultra-high-definition (4K), high-definition (PAL), and 4K PAL video recording are all possible with certain iPhone models.

- Select Camera > Settings > Record Video.

To play a video on your iPhone, choose it from the list of supported file types and frame rates.

Please be aware that video files are much bigger as frame rates increase and resolutions increase.

A lot of places in Europe, Africa, Asia, and South America utilize a video standard called PAL on their televisions.

Switch to Active Mode

Improved video stabilization is available in Action mode on the iPhone 14 and iPhone 15 models. To activate Action mode, tap the button that says "Action Mode Off" at the top of the screen.

The iPhone is now lying flat on the table. The camera is active and set to record videos. You'll find the Flash player's toggle switch in the lower-left corner. Toggle switches for changing the video's resolution and frame rate, as well as the Action button, can be found in the upper left corner of the screen, to the left of the Camera Controls button. The toggle for "Action" is now active. The Camera Chooser Back-Facing button, Record, and Photo/Video Viewer buttons are located on the right side of the device. Someone is sprinting in the viewfinder.

- To reiterate, action mode performs best in well-lit areas. Settings > Camera > Record Video > Action Mode Lower Light will enable Action mode for usage in low light. The highest resolution you can take at while in action mode is 2.8K.

USE YOUR IPHONE CAMERA TO SHOOT QUICKTAKE

When shooting video, "QuickTake" refers to the "Photo" setting. You may lock the Record button in place and keep snapping images all during your QuickTake video recording.

To begin shooting a QuickTake video, open the Camera app and tap and hold the Shutter button.

Hands-free recording is enabled by swiping the Shutter button to the right and releasing it beyond the lock.

Below the camera's viewfinder, you'll find both the record and shutter buttons, respectively.

To get a closer look at your subject, just squeeze the screen up if you're recording manually, or swipe up if you're going hands-free.

Remove a recording by tapping the Record button.

In this shot, the subject occupies the bulk of the frame in the camera's viewfinder. The Shutter button, located at the bottom of the screen, slides to the right while a QuickTake movie is being started. The video's clock may be seen at the very top of the display.

To begin recording a QuickTake video while in the Photo mode, press and hold the volume up or volume down button.

QuickTake videos may be seen in the Photos app by tapping on the thumbnail.

Make a time-lapse video.

In Slo-mo mode, your video will record normally, and the slow-motion effect will only become apparent when you play back the video. Your video's slow-motion effects may be set to begin and end at any point you like.

Select the slow-motion option in the camera's menu.

You can use the front-facing camera to capture slow-motion video on the iPhone 11, 12, 13, 14, and 15 by tapping the Camera Chooser Back-Facing button.

- To begin recording, push either volume button or tap the Record button.
- While recording, you may snap a still image by tapping the Shutter button.
- To stop recording, tap the Record button or use the volume controls.

To make just a certain segment of a movie play at slow motion while the remainder continues at normal speed, choose the thumbnail and then select Edit. Drag the vertical bars under the frame viewer to set the start and end points of the slow-motion playback.

Both the slow-motion frame rate and resolution are model-specific. Navigate to the Settings menu > Camera > Record Slo-mo to adjust the slow-motion recording options.

Toggling between different resolutions and frame rates when recording is a breeze with this helpful hint. See Adjust the frame rate and quality of your videos with the click of a button.

Time-lapse video recording

Time-lapse videos are created by taking pictures at regular intervals to show the progression of an event over a period of time, such as the setting of the sun or the flow of traffic.

The Time-lapse setting may be found in the Camera menu.

Position your iPhone where you anticipate action to occur.

To begin recording, hit the Record button to stop recording, tap the button again.

If you're filming a time-lapse movie on an iPhone 12 or later, you may improve the quality and exposure by using a tripod.

RECORD PRORES VIDEOS WITH YOUR IPHONE CAMERA

Video captured and edited in Camera may be saved in the better quality and less compressed ProRes format on models that are compatible.

Every camera, including the one at the front, can record in ProRes. Cinematic, Time-lapse, and Slow-mo modes do not support ProRes.

Keep in mind that file sizes increase with ProRes video.

Configure ProRes

- Turn on Apple ProRes in the camera's settings by selecting Settings > Camera > Formats.
- To start recording in ProRes, launch the camera, switch to the video mode, and finally, hit the ProRes Off button.
- To begin recording, push either volume button or tap the Record button.

You may squeeze to zoom in or out when the back camera is filming, as well as press to focus.Slide the dial for finer-grained zoom adjustment, or use the 5x, 1x, 2x, 3x, and 5x buttons to quickly swap between lenses (depending on your model).

- To stop recording, tap the Record button or use the volume controls.
- To disable ProRes, choose the corresponding button.

Up to 4K recording at 30 fps is supported in ProRes. When using an external storage device, the iPhone 15 Pro and iPhone 15 Pro Max are capable of recording in 4K at 60 frames per second.

Only the iPhone 15 Pro 128 GB model may record in 4K at up to 60 fps when linked to an external storage device that supports that format. All other 128 GB iPhone models are limited to recording at 1080p at 30 fps. Check out the page on Apple's support site titled "About Apple ProRes on iPhone" for further details.

Color coding may be selected for ProRes recordings.

The iPhone 15 Pro and 15 Pro Max allow users to capture video in ProRes with a selection of color encoding options, including HDR, SDR, and Log.

- To enable Apple ProRes, choose it from the Formats menu under Settings > Camera.
- Select ProRes Encoding and then HDR, SDR, or Log.

CHANGE ADVANCED CAMERA SETTINGS ON IPHONE

Find out how to use the camera's more complex settings to take pictures faster, add special effects and filters, and see things that are normally hidden from view.

Modify the Resolution of the Primary Camera

The primary camera on iPhone 15 models has a default resolution of 24 megapixels. The resolution may be changed from 12 MP to 24 MP to 48 MP.

- Select either 12 MP or 24 MP under the "Photo Mode" submenu of "Settings" on your device.

Resolution Control or ProRAW & Resolution Control (depending on your model) may be activated in the camera's settings menu under "Formats" to enable 48 megapixel capture.

After activating ProRAW & Resolution Control on either the iPhone 15 Pro or iPhone 15 Pro Max, you'll be prompted to choose a default format through the Pro Default menu. Launch the camera app and use the format selector toggle at the app's top. To change formats, touch and hold the toggle.

Toggle the Outside View On/Off

- On compatible devices, the camera preview will show you what's beyond the frame if you have a wider-angle lens installed in the camera system. By default, "View Outside the Frame" is on.
- View Outside the Frame may be disabled by selecting Settings > Camera > View Outside the Frame.

Prioritize Quicker Fire by Toggling It On and Off.

When you touch the Shutter button fast, the Prioritize Faster Shooting option adjusts the picture processing so that you can take more shots. Faster shooting is prioritized by default.

- Prioritize Faster Shooting may be disabled by selecting Settings > Camera > Disable Prioritize Faster Shooting.

Flip the switch for lens correction.

When enabled, the Lens Correction option improves the appearance of selfies and ultra wide shots produced with compatible devices. By default, lens correction will be on.

- Lens Correction may be disabled by selecting Settings > Camera > Lens Correction.

Toggle Scene Detection On/Off

The Scene Detection feature on iPhone 12 models automatically determines what you're photographing and then applies an effect specifically designed to highlight relevant details. The scene detector is on by default.

- Settings > Camera > Scene Detection Off will disable Scene Detection.

ADJUST THE SHUTTER VOLUME ON YOUR IPHONE CAMERA

The iPhone's Camera shutter sound may be muted or changed using the Ring/Silent switch on the device's side.

Adjust the shutter sound volume in the camera's Photo mode.

Activate the camera's photo mode.

- On adjust the volume, launch Control Center and use the slider on the right.
- A bottom-up swipe will take you back to Camera.

When taking Live Photos, the shutter will not produce a sound (except in some nations and locations).

Turn off the camera's shutter

- Turn off the iPhone's shutter sound by toggling the Ring/Silent switch on the device's side. To activate Silent mode on an iPhone, flip the Ring/Silent switch to the orange position. Simply turning the switch off will restore normal operation.

Instead of a dedicated Ring/Silent toggle, the iPhone 15 Pro and 15 Pro Max include an Action button. In addition to its other uses, the Action button toggles Silent mode.

Important: The shutter sound cannot be muted in all places.

CHAPTER FOUR

HOW TO ENABLE/DISABLE HDR ON IPHONE

All the way up to 4K HDR at 30 frames per second may be recorded in Cinematic mode with Smart HDR 4 on the iPhone 14 Pro and iPhone 14 Pro Max. Using the Auto adjust toggle and HDR Video Recording, users of the TrueDepth Camera with Smart HDR 4 may take powerful selfies. Here's how you use the iPhone's camera settings to toggle Smart HDR on and off.

In low light or night mode, High Dynamic Range (HRD) photography takes numerous photographs with a wide range of exposures.

Disabling High Dynamic Range on an iPhone

All images taken on an iPhone 12 or later are taken in HDR by default. Through the Photos app's sharing options, we can have a look at it on your iPhone. By selecting this option, the display will be automatically calibrated to show the full dynamic range of HDR images.

To check out some stunning images, open the Settings app, go to Photos, and tap View Full HDR (Turn on the switch).

Check out HDR Images on Your iPhone

However, in the iPhone 12 and later, we can turn off Smart HDR for Video. as this lesson explains.

For iOS 11 and older iPhones,

- Launch the iPhone's Settings application.
- To access the iPhone 2's smart hdr settings, open the Settings app, scroll down the screen, and hit the Camera tab. Move the cursor to the camera icon and click it.
- Look for the " HDR " option and turn it on under the "HDR" subheading. The newest iPhone model, the 11.

Enable HDR on iPhone

The HDR skillfully combines the most desirable qualities of many exposures into a single image. Look at the standard picture as well as the HDR one.

By Default, Smart HDR Is On on the iPhone 12, iPhone 13, and iPhone 14. This HDR video sets a new standard for accurate color reproduction and dynamic range.

Once HDR is on, you may toggle it to Off, On, or Automatic inside the Camera app.

HDR photography is always enabled, so you may take pictures in any lighting.

Turns the HDR picture quality off forcibly.

When using the Camera app, your iPhone will turn on and off automatically based on the conditions it detects in the surrounding area.

Turn on/Off iPhone HDR Video

If you own an iPhone 12 or later, you may use these toggles to enable and disable the ability to record HRD video. If you want more dynamic range and accurate colors while recording video on your iPhone, you may activate Dolby Vision HDR.

- Turn on your iPhone's "HDR Video" feature by going to the Settings > Camera > Record Video menu.

iPhone HDR video recording.

Video Captured in HDR Mode and Annotated in the Photos App,

Turn off or disable HDR on your iPhone

Without changing any of the camera's settings, we may disable HDR photography.

The iPhone's HDR photography feature may be temporarily turned off.

- Fire up the Camera app on your iPhone. Select "Off" from the HDR menu by tapping on it.
- go to your iPhone's Settings > Camera > Record Video > HDR. The next step is to disable HDR.

For the iPhone 8, 8 Plus, and X, Auto HDR is available.

The functionality of Auto HDR on older iPhone devices is identical to that of newer iPhone models. That makes advantage of Apple's powerful neural processor. Making a machine-learning challenge in low-light photography.

- Go to "Settings" > "Camera" > "Auto HDR (Disable or Enable it)" to activate or deactivate the feature.

CHANGE THE CAMERA'S VIDEO RECORDING SETTINGS ON IPHONE

Camera's frame rate defaults to 30 fps (frames per second). The available options for frame rate and video resolution on an iPhone are device-specific. Video files become bigger as frame rates and resolutions increase.

On-screen toggles make it simple to switch between different video qualities and frame rates.

The video's frame rate and resolution may be toggled easily.

In Video mode, you may quickly switch between the iPhone's supported video resolutions and frame rates by using the toggles at the screen's top.

Toggling between HD and 4K recording and 24, 25, 30, or 60 fps in Video mode is as easy as tapping the appropriate fast toggles in the upper right corner.

In Cinematic mode on the iPhone 14 and iPhone 15, you may quickly shift between HD, 4K, 24, 25, and 30 frames per second.

Set the frame rate to automatic

By automatically dropping to 24 frames per second, an iPhone may enhance video quality in low-light conditions.

- Select Camera > Record Video from the menu that appears after going into Settings.
- Select Auto FPS, and then use it with either 30- or 60-frame-per-second video.

Engage Low-Light FPS Auto.

Toggle between mono and stereo recording

The iPhone's stereo sound is the result of using several microphones.

- Select Camera > Settings > Record Stereo Sound to disable stereo recording.

Switch on and off HDR playback

Supported iPhone models may capture video in High Dynamic Range (HDR) and share HDR films with devices running iOS 13.4, iPadOS 13.4, macOS 10.15.4 or later.

Disabling HDR recording is as simple as going to the camera's settings and selecting "Record Video" from the drop-down menu.

Lock and unlock the camera.

The Lock Camera option prohibits the automatic switching between cameras on the iPhone 13, iPhone 14, and iPhone 15 models when shooting video. By default, camera locking is disabled.

- Settings > Camera > Record Video is where you'll find Lock Camera.

Activate and deactivate Enhanced Stabilization.

When shooting in Video mode or Cinematic mode on an iPhone 14 or 15, the Enhanced stability setting zooms in significantly to give enhanced stability. By default, Enhanced Stabilization is enabled.

- To disable Enhanced Stabilization, tap the Settings icon, then Camera, and finally Record Video.

Lock White Balance On/Off Switch

If you want more consistent color capture regardless of the lighting circumstances, you may lock the white balance on your iPhone when recording video.

- You may activate Lock White Balance in your device's settings by navigating to Camera > Record Video > Settings.

HOW TO ENABLE AND USE LIVE TEXT ON YOUR IPHONE

You can teach your phone to read text from images, web pages, and the Camera app if you familiarize yourself with Live Text.

Apple introduced iOS 15 with a plethora of new features at its annual developer conference. Live Text, which uses machine learning, is one of the most notable new features.

What is live text?

Machine learning is used in Live Text's text recognition functionality. In many ways, this is the iOS equivalent of Google Lens.

Live Text eliminates the need to manually enter text from the physical world. Simply place your iPhone's camera over a picture containing text, and it will read the text for you. In addition, you have options on what to do with the detected text.

Better still, you can use Live content with either handwritten or typed content. Learn more about Live Text and its capabilities here.

Help and Availability with Real-Time Text

Live Text has several benefits, but it is only compatible with iOS 15 and iPadOS 15. Live Text, according to Apple, is limited to iPhones and iPads powered by the 7nm A12 Bionic CPU or later. All iPads and iPhones introduced in 2018 and after are covered by this. Macs released in 2018 or after provide support for Live Text as well.

Tips for Enabling Real-Time Text

- Open the iPhone or iPad's Settings menu.
- Find the Camera app by looking under "Apps."
- Live Text may be activated in the camera settings. If the switch is in the green position, then Live Text is active.
- Activated "Live Text" function
- Now that Live Text has been activated, let's check out some of its uses.

Guide to Using Live Text

Live Text is a feature of iOS 15 and iPadOS 15 that may be used in a variety of situations. Moreover, you may find alternative applications in other contexts.

The main functions of Live Text include translation, searching for a word or phrase, and copying text.

The text may be interacted with in several ways, such phoning a phone, sending an email, etc.

Starting with the Photos app, we'll go through the fundamentals of utilizing Live Text in various contexts down below.

How to use Live Text in the Photos App

Live Text allows you to interact with any text superimposed over an image. Here's how to utilize Live Text on a picture including handwritten or typed text:

A photo album may be accessed by launching the app.

- Pick a picture with text and tap it.
- Select the scanner-shaped Live Text symbol in the right-hand corner. All text that can be read in a picture will be highlighted by Live Text.
- Select several words by tapping and holding the screen as you drag your finger. To pick all of the highlighted text, choose pick All from the highlights menu.
- Choose an option for processing the text in the window that appears. Several programs allow you to do things like copy, translate, research, and distribute the material.

Live Text is a tool for selecting text from photographs.

Using Live Text on iOS 15 and making a selection

The Camera App's Live Text Function and How to Use It

The camera app itself has support for Live Text. Therefore, there is no need to snap a photo. Texts in photos may be scanned and used for further processing.

Instructions on how to utilize Live Text inside the Camera app are provided below.

- Open up the Camera software.
- Shoot whatever written material you like.
- Choose the "Live Text" button. When you move the mouse over your target, a menu will appear so you may interact with it. Before you touch the Live Text icon, make sure the text you wish to copy is completely encased in the yellow brackets. This is because while using Live Text, you can only choose text that is included inside the frames.
- Select the text by swiping or tapping.

From the highlighted options, choose the one that best suits your needs.

Locate on-screen text prompts using Live Text targeting.

Email addresses, phone numbers, and URLs all allow for instantaneous communication. To visit the linked website, for instance, just press the link and your default web browser will load the address.

A Guide to using Live Text with Every Other App

Live Text is not limited to the Camera or Photos applications; it may be used in a variety of programs. You may use Live Text to inject text from the webcam into any input area.

- If you press and hold an input field inside your note, the standard iOS popover will appear.
- Choose the icon labeled "Live Text." In this case, iOS will divide the screen in half, showing you a minimized version of your note on the left and the Camera app on the right.
- To copy text, just aim the camera at it.
- To complete, click the Insert button.

Using Live Text to include real-world text into your notes

Your message will now include the image's text. Live Text's system-wide availability opens up a world of possibilities for the iPhone and iPad.

Increase Efficiency with Real-Time Text

Live Text is a great time-saving tool since it allows you to take notes as quickly as possible. Photos have always been a quick method of data collection, but they lack the ease of Live Text. No longer will you have to retype the contact number after shooting a photo. Furthermore, nowadays, taking a photograph is completely unnecessary.

CHAPTER FIVE

HOW TO READ QR CODES ON IPHONE

To begin, let's establish that this is, in fact, a QR code. QR codes are a kind of machine-readable code that can store more data than its one-dimensional counterpart, the barcode. This is because QR codes are two-dimensional—the camera on an Apple iPhone 15 Plus must scan the code from both the left and right sides.

The Apple iPhone 15 Plus has a 48-megapixel, f/1.6, 26mm (wide), 1.0-micron (m) dual-pixel phase detection autofocus (PDAF) and sensor-shift optical image stabilization (OIS) camera, and a 12-megapixel, f/2.4, 13-millimeter (mm) 120-degree (degrees) ultrawide-angle camera.

The code reader on the iPhone 15 Plus is built into the camera's software, so there's no need to download a separate app to read or scan QR codes.

Time required: 2 minutes on average.

To begin with

- The built-in "Camera" software on the Apple iPhone 15 Plus may be used to read or capture QR codes; to access it, just tap the camera icon on the home screen.
- Using the 48-megapixel, f/1.6, 26mm (wide), 1.0-micron, dual-pixel phase detection autofocus (PDAF), sensor-shift optical image stabilization (OIS) and 12-megapixel, f/2.4, 13mm, 120-degree (ultrawide) rear camera on the Apple iPhone 15 Plus, we aim the camera at the QR code we want to read, making sure it appears correctly focused and content within the yellow square or at least within the viewing space.

Since there is no "up" or "down" in a QR code, it doesn't matter which way we approach it as long as the complete code is shown on the screen of an Apple iPhone 15 Plus.

- Scan a QR code using your iPhone 15

Most QR codes contain a web address, so the iPhone 15 Plus will prompt us to open "Safari" or our default web browser once it has decoded the code.

When we get a notice, we open the link or take the action by clicking on it.

➢ Open the QR Code

Following these easy instructions, we were able to successfully scan QR codes using our Apple iPhone 15 Plus. QR codes often lead to websites, where users may look up information such as a restaurant's menu or a promotional coupon.

WHERE TO FIND PHOTOS AND VIDEOS SHARED WITH YOU ON YOUR IPHONE

Discovering media that others have shared with you is a breeze on your iPhone.

You, the readers, play a vital role in keeping MUO online and free for everyone. We may get compensation if you make a purchase after clicking on one of our affiliate links. Learn More.

A powerful new feature in iOS 15 makes it simpler to locate material that other people have shared with you. Images, movies, podcasts, and webpages all fit under this category. And it will appear in the applications you typically use for that particular content kind. Photos and videos are the most popular items to post, so that's what we'll be looking at today.

Photos and movies that have been shared with you may be found in a special area of your library labeled "Shared with You." Everything you need to know is listed here.

In the Shared with You area of your photographs app, you can simply locate any photographs or videos that have been sent to you via the Messages app.

- Simply go to the Photos section, choose the For You button, and then hit Shared with You.
- Make sure the function is activated, however. To enable this feature for photos, go to Settings > Messages > Shared with You. Simply return to this page and flip the Photos switch to "off" to disable the feature.
- On an iPhone, go to General > Messages.

Options for Sharing Messages with You Have Been Posted Here

Taking Part in the Media Others Share With You

Content that has been Shared with You may be used in a number of ways. Selecting a picture with a tap takes it into full screen, where you may edit, share, or save it. To see everything that has been sent to you, choose See all.

- Select Library, then press the All Photos option. A little speech bubble will show in the bottom left corner of thumbnails of images and videos in which you were present or in which you made an appearance. To save, remove, or share an image, just touch its thumbnail.
- You can do the same thing with photographs right from inside Messages. If you click the icon next to the picture, you'll be prompted to download it. When it disappears, it implies you've successfully added the picture to your collection.

Download Picture from Messages Button

Instead, you'll see the sender's profile picture or initials and the words "From [Name]" superimposed on top of any images they send you. When you tap this, Messages will open so you may respond to the thread.

Messages Now Allows You to Respond to Posted Photos

It's important to remember that erasing a discussion also removes any attached media you didn't preserve.

Get all your needs met with With Shared with You, all of the photos and videos your friends have sent you are automatically gathered in one place—the Photos app—saving you the trouble of searching through many threads to locate what you're looking for. And it's not just for Photos; the functionality works everywhere, making it much simpler to find what you need, when you need it.

SET UP ICLOUD PHOTOS ON ALL YOUR DEVICES

You may access iCloud Photos on iCloud.com, as well as on your iOS devices, Mac, Apple TV, PC, and Windows computer. See Keep your images and videos up-to-date in iCloud to get a feel for what you can accomplish with iCloud images.

It's important to remember to use the same Apple ID on all of your gadgets. Your photographs and videos won't be available on devices that aren't linked in to your Apple ID or have iCloud photographs disabled.

Create an iCloud Photo Library on your iOS device.

- To access the Photos section of iCloud on your iOS device, tap Settings > [your name] > iCloud.

- Put this device into sync mode.

The Photos tab in iCloud Preferences. The iPhone is ready to sync at this time.

Activate Photos in iCloud.

The Photos app uploads everything on your iPhone to iCloud, including videos. In addition, you may see the films and pictures that have been uploaded to iCloud Photos on your mobile device.

- Launch the Photos app, and then choose Library to see your iCloud Photo Library. The media you are seeing is pulled from iCloud Photos.
- To see how far along your picture sync is, just look down at the bottom of your screen.
- Using iCloud Photos with Your iPod touch (iOS 15 or Earlier)

Prepare your Mac for iCloud Photo Streaming

- Choose one of the following actions in the Mac Photos app:
- Using macOS 13 or later Select iCloud from the drop-down menu under Photo Settings.

- Prior to macOS Version 12: Select iCloud from the Photos > Preferences menu.

Choose to upload photos to iCloud.

Your Mac's Photos library will sync to iCloud automatically. Your Mac may now access the photographs and videos you have saved in iCloud photographs.

If you have numerous picture libraries on your Mac, please be aware that iCloud photographs will only sync the photographs and videos in the System picture Library.

Launch the Photos app, and then choose Library from the app's sidebar to see your iCloud Photos. The media you are seeing is pulled from iCloud Photos.

To see how far along your picture sync is, just look down at the bottom of your screen.

Use iCloud photographs to save photographs in iCloud in the Mac's Photos User Guide for further information on how to upload and manage your digital images in the cloud.

Prepare your Apple TV for iCloud Photo Streaming

- Launch the Apple TV's Settings application.
- To access your account, go to Users and Accounts.
- Select iCloud, and then enable iCloud Photos.
- Launch the Photos app and go to the Photos section of the main menu to see your iCloud Photos. The media you are seeing is pulled from iCloud Photos.

Install iCloud Photo Library on a Windows PC.

- In case you haven't already, install iCloud on your Windows computer.
- Select Photos in iCloud for Windows.
- Choose to upload photos to iCloud.
- To activate further settings, go to your camera's settings by clicking the gear icon.
- To finish, choose Done and then Apply.

Open File Explorer and choose iCloud Photos from the left pane to see your iCloud Photo Library.

Double-click iCloud Photos if it isn't already selected after clicking Pictures in the sidebar.

Check out the iCloud for Windows User Guide sections on "Download and view iCloud Photos on your Windows computer" and "Add photos and videos to iCloud from your Windows computer" for additional information on using iCloud Photos on your Windows computer.

Upload Images to iCloud.com

Photos and movies stored in iCloud may be viewed on any device with a web browser, including mobile devices and computers.

SET UP AND USE ICLOUD PHOTOS

Using the photographs app in tandem with iCloud Photos ensures that all of your photographs and videos are always in sync across your iOS devices, Mac, Apple TV, and iCloud.com.

Functioning of iCloud Photos

With iCloud Photos, all of your photos and videos are stored in the cloud and can be accessed from any of your devices at any time. Any adjustments you make to your collection on one gadget will reflect across all of them. There are tabs for each year, each month, each day, and "All Photos" to house all of your media. In addition, your People and Pets and Memories are always up to date. That way, you may easily locate the desired memory, relative, or friend.

All of your high-resolution still images and video clips will remain in their original forms on iCloud.

Formats include slow motion, time lapse, 4K video, and Live Photos, as well as the more common HEIF, JPEG, RAW, PNG, GIF, TIFF, HEVC, and MP4, may all be captured with an iPhone or iPad. The devices record in the high efficiency image and video formats (HEIF and HEVC), respectively. The time it takes for your images and videos to appear on all of your devices and iCloud.com might vary based on the speed of your internet connection.

Enable iCloud Photo Library

Set up iCloud on every machine you own and use the same Apple ID to access it.

- Using an iOS device, such as an iPhone or iPad
- Navigate to > > [your name> > Settings.
- Select "iCloud" from the menu.
- Select Photos, then toggle the button underneath Sync this [device].

Using a Mac

- Select "System Preferences" or "System Settings" from the Apple menu.
- Select Apple ID from the menu.
- Select Photos from the iCloud submenu that appears.

- To sync this Mac, flip the switch.

The 4K and HD models of Apple TV

Activate Users and Accounts by selecting Settings.

Go with iCloud.

- Activate Photos in iCloud.
- Using a Windows-based personal computer

The repercussions of modifying or erasing pictures

All of your devices will update automatically whenever you add, modify, or remove media.

Any changes you make will reflect across all of your devices.

Photos on your iPhone, iPad, or Mac will update on all of your other devices, including your Apple TV, as soon as you save your changes. You can edit photos on your iPhone and see the results when you open them in iPhoto on your Mac. All of your original photographs and videos are safely kept in iCloud, so you can always go back and undo any edits you may have done.

Remove pictures from all of your gadgets.

Photos and movies deleted from one iCloud Photos-enabled device are also removed from all other devices. You have 30 days to check the Recently Deleted folder in case you remove anything by mistake. The information is then permanently removed.

Get backups of your precious pictures and clips.

Turning on iCloud Photos triggers an instant upload of all of your media to the cloud service. To be safe, you should make additional copies of your library outside of iCloud. Follow these instructions to save local copies of your media to your computer. Alternatively, you may transfer your collection to a computer.

- ➤ Save your media files to your computer from iCloud.com.
- ➤ Visit the Photos tab on iCloud.com.
- ➤ Pick out the films and pictures you want to save.

A high-resolution download option is available by clicking the download button in the window's upper-right corner. You may also go to More Download Options by clicking the More button.

Choose Most Compatible if you want to download in the format most suited to your device, such as JPEG or H.264. Choose Unmodified Original to get your stuff exactly as it was when it was taken or imported.

- To get the download, just click.

Get media from your iOS device and save it locally.

- Launch the Photos app and choose some media to see.
- Use the button to share it.
- Select the target device from the list that appears once you tap AirDrop. Find out how to make the most of AirDrop.

Get media files off of your Mac.

- Launch the Photos program on your Mac.
- Pick out some media to see.
- Simply drop the files onto your desktop or To use AirDrop, right-click and choose Share.

Make sure you have adequate space for everything.

Your iCloud storage and device storage are both used by the photographs and videos stored in iCloud photographs. You may save as many pictures and movies as you like as long as you have adequate room in iCloud and on your smartphone.

Get additional space in iCloud

The first 5GB of storage space on iCloud is free when you join up. Upgrade to iCloud+ to have access to more storage and other benefits.

If you're using an iPad or iPhone with iOS 17 or later, you may access your iCloud settings to look for unnecessary media and erase it.

Figure out how to declutter your life

Optimization of Storage Capacity will be activated

All of your photographs and videos will always be stored in their full, original quality in iCloud photographs. You may enable optimization of storage space on your device.

When the Optimize Storage setting is on, iCloud Photos takes care of keeping your library at the optimal size for your device. Your smartphone only stores a compressed copy of your media; the originals live in iCloud. Only when you're running low on storage space does your library begin to be streamlined, beginning with the photographs and movies you seldom see. When you require access to the original photographs and movies, you may do so over Wi-Fi or mobile data.

With Download Originals enabled, iCloud photographs will always save your device's original, high-resolution photographs and videos alongside their iCloud counterparts.

Using an iOS device, such as an iPhone or iPad

- Select [your name] > iCloud from the Settings menu.
- Select Images.
- Select Optimize [device] Storage from the menu.

Using a Mac

- To launch Photos, choose Photos from the app's main menu.
- Just go to somewhere like Settings or Preferences.
- Select a backup option in iCloud by clicking that tab.

Hold off on Syncing Your Library to iCloud

The time it takes for your photographs and videos to upload to iCloud once you switch on iCloud photographs is affected by the number of files you have and the speed of your internet connection. If you have a lot of media files to transfer, the upload process might take longer than normal. You may check the upload's progress and pause it for 24 hours.

To see all photos on your iPhone or iPad, use the Photos app and go to the Library menu. If you want to see it, go to the very bottom of the page.

- Launch the Photos program on your Mac. From the sidebar, choose Library, and then from the toolbar's tabs, choose All Photos. Click the Pause button at the very bottom of your picture gallery.

CHAPTER SIX

HOW TO PRINT A PAPER COPY OR A PDF FROM AN IPHONE

The iOS features AirPrint and Print to PDF, which allow you to easily print paper copies or digital PDFs from your iOS device, make document management a breeze.

Both an iPhone and an iPad are displayed vertically on a kitchen counter, with natural light streaming in via a window on the left. The iPhone's Print Options screen displays the printer's name, the number of pages to print, whether or not to print on both sides of the paper, and what paper size to use. Two pages featuring a corgi are previewed at the bottom. The iPad also has a screen that allows you to print a page, although no printer is preselected.

Shipping labels, bulletin board fliers, emailing your boss, and posting prank memes in coworkers' cubes are all examples of printing tasks that are still difficult to automate in today's paperless society. In a day when most tasks can be completed on a mobile device, the ability to print without first using a computer is a welcome convenience.

Apple's AirPrint wireless printing function has been adopted by several printer makers, making it one of the simplest ways to print from a smartphone. If you know where to look, Apple also provides a simple method for creating PDF documents in place of a printed copy. Both will be shown in this article.

Using AirPrint to Print

Note that not all printer capabilities will work while using AirPrint, but you should still be able to choose the desired number of copies, range, paper size, orientation, and scaling.

To get started, you'll need access to a wireless or network printer that is compatible with Apple's driverless printing technology, AirPrint. If you need a printer but don't have one yet, here's some advice on picking the best one out there. There is a good probability that your wireless printer already supports AirPrint if you bought it within the previous five years (or up to ten years in the case of HP). In addition to AirPrint, several printer manufacturers provide their own apps that allow you to print documents from your mobile device or from the manufacturer's own cloud service.

To proceed, check that both your iPhone and your printer are linked to the same wireless network. You may also use AirPrint from your iPhone by connecting the printer directly to your wireless network via an ethernet connection, if your printer has one. To print from an iPhone, you may need to ask your IT staff to enable the service in a business setting.

Putting anything to paper has finally arrived.

Launch the app that has the content you want to print, such as an email, an attachment, Safari, a file in the Files app, a picture, etc.

Open the share sheet by tapping the Share button, then find the Print option by scrolling down. The Print option may be found in a different menu in certain applications. If you want to print an email message, you may do so by tapping the Reply button and then scrolling down to the Print option in the list of reply choices that appears.

If there isn't already a default printer listed on the Print Options screen, choose one.

You may now customize your print job by selecting the number of copies, the number of pages per copy, whether or not to print on both sides of the paper, and other parameters.

You may just press Print and send it on its way.

The print queue / order status may be seen by either double-clicking the home button (iPhone with Touch ID) or by swiping up from the bottom of the screen (iPhone with Face ID or iPad) to access the App Switcher. If the print job hasn't been finished yet, you may cancel it here as well.

Only while printing is in progress does the print queue show up in the App Switcher.

While the print is still in progress, you may tap for a print summary and to cancel the print job.

To Save as a PDF

When compared to macOS, which has had a prominent Save as PDF option for years, iOS's treatment of printing to PDF as an Easter egg is astounding. iOS doesn't have a dedicated print to PDF button, so you'll need to zoom in on the page to see the choice.

Follow the steps above to access the Print Options menu for the document or web page you want to save as a PDF.

Zoom in on the printed document preview by pinching the screen. It will come at you quickly, like switching to a new level in a video game.

The file is currently being viewed in PDF format. To make sure the content you seek is shown accurately, you may use the screen's page navigation tools, zoom feature, and text search function.

- Select the share icon located in the bottom left corner.
- To save the file to a specific location, choose Save to Files; to transfer it straight to someone else, select another app such as Mail, Messages, or AirDrop.

HOW TO PRINT EMAILS FROM YOUR IPHONE

Notifications for the iPhone's Mail App

If you use Mail or Gmail on your iPhone, printing an email is a breeze.

If you have a wireless printer set up in close proximity to your iPhone, you can effortlessly print emails from your phone.

Whether you use Apple's default Mail app or a third-party software like Gmail, you can print emails from your iPhone.

To print from an iPhone, both the iPhone and the printer must be connected to the same Wi-Fi network.

The conveniences provided by modern technology continue to multiply. In the past, printing required a cumbersome physical connection between the printer and computer. You would have to transfer the file to a computer before printing it from your phone.

In less time than it took me to type the last phrase, you can print a picture, note, or email from your iPhone to a wireless printer connected to the same Wi-Fi network.

Knowing where to touch on an iPhone will allow you to print emails.

The Mail app on the iPhone explains how to print an email.

To print an email, one must first locate and open it.

- Select the arrow icon located in the right-hand corner of the display.
- Any email in a chain may be printed by choosing the most recent one, or you can choose a specific one by tapping on it. Business Insider/Steven John
- Once you get to the bottom of the menu, choose "Print."
- decide the printer you'll be using.

- Make any necessary adjustments, and then click the "Print" button in the upper-right corner.
- Locate the message you'd want to print in the Gmail app and touch on it.
- Click the ellipses (...) next to the sender's name.
- Keep in mind that the three dots at the top of the screen conceal yet another printing choice. Business Insider/Steven John
- Select your wireless printer by tapping "Print" and then "AirPrint."
- Then, when you've double-checked your options, you may click "Print."

CHAPTER SEVEN

GET STARTED WITH FACETIME ON IPHONE

Find out how to make video calls using the Wi-Fi or cellular connection and the FaceTime app. You may do anything from work out together to watch a movie or TV program over a FaceTime conversation.

The FaceTime settings window, including the toggle to enable or disable the app and the Apple ID input area.

Connect using FaceTime.

To activate FaceTime, choose Settings > FaceTime from the main menu. Put your Apple ID or phone number where it says "You can be reached by FaceTime at," if you haven't previously.

Communicate over FaceTime.

To initiate a FaceTime call, launch the program, choose New FaceTime, and then add the contact(s) you want to speak with. You can make a visual call with the FaceTime button, or an audio call via the Call button (not accessible in all countries and regions). The maximum number of participants per call is 32.

Using Messages or Mail, you can set up a call with someone who doesn't have an Apple device and then email them a link to the call. Launch FaceTime and choose the Create Link option to get going.

While the other person's picture takes up the majority of the screen, the caller's image displays in a little rectangle in the bottom right. You may access Live Photo, Effects, and the Reverse Camera by tapping the corresponding icons at the screen's bottom. Above the video are buttons labeled "Speaker," "Camera," "Mute," "Share Content," and "End." The name or Apple ID of the person you're chatting with appears at the very top of the interface.

Make use of FaceTime's settings

You can use the FaceTime controls to do things like snap a Live Photo during a conversation, mute your microphone, or adjust the volume of your speaker. To access the options, touch the screen if necessary.

Sharing video from an Apple TV+ device over a FaceTime chat using the SharePlay feature. The content creator is shown in the thumbnail, the video takes up the remainder of the screen, and the controls appear over the top of the video.

Take turns watching, listening, and playing

Start sharing media during a FaceTime chat by tapping the Share Content button (or tapping the screen if you don't see the Share Content button) under the FaceTime controls.

MAKE A GROUP FACETIME CALL ON IPHONE

Group FaceTime calls in the FaceTime app support up to 32 people at once (but this feature isn't accessible in all areas).

Initiate a FaceTime conference call

- Select New FaceTime from FaceTime's menu bar.
- In the first blank, enter the names or phone numbers of the persons you like to contact.
- Alternatively, you may launch Contacts and add individuals that way by tapping the Add Contact icon. You may also use the recommended contacts from your call log.

The FaceTime button initiates a visual call, while the Call button initiates an audio call.

A tile for each player is shown on the screen. A tile is made more noticeable when a participant makes a comment about it, either orally or via the use of sign language, or when you press the tile. Overflow tiles line up toward the bottom of the screen. To locate an absent contributor, just swipe down the column. (If no suitable picture is available, the participant's initials may be used instead.)

Please refer to View participants in a grid layout in FaceTime on iPhone if you like to view the photographs of the participants grouped in a grid.

- Turn off Speaking below Automatic Prominence in Settings > FaceTime to avoid the tile of the person speaking or signing from being more prominent during a Group FaceTime chat.

The group chat in Messages may be converted into a FaceTime call.

During an iMessage discussion with many participants, you have the option to initiate a group FaceTime call.

- Select the FaceTime icon located in the upper right corner of the iMessage window.
- Just choose one of the following:

- To listen to someone using FaceTime, choose the audio icon.
- Select FaceTime Video.

Join a call with another person

During a FaceTime call, anybody may invite someone else to join at any moment.

If the FaceTime controls aren't already visible, you may bring them up by tapping the screen while on a FaceTime chat; once they're there, press the More Info button at the controls' top; finally, hit Add People.

Input the desired contact's name, Apple ID, or phone number in the top box.

You may also use the Contacts list by tapping the Add Contact button.

- Select the +People button.
- Join a FaceTime conference call

You'll get a notice if someone asks you to a Group FaceTime call, and you may accept or refuse the call at that time. See Get a call over FaceTime.

Abandon a FaceTime conference call

- Select Leave to end a conference call at any moment.
- If there are still at least two people on the call, it will continue.

VIEW PARTICIPANTS IN A GRID LAYOUT IN FACETIME ON IPHONE

If you're on a FaceTime chat with four individuals or more, everyone will appear as identically sized tiles in a grid. The tile of the current speaker is immediately illuminated so that everyone can see who is talking. (Some tiles may seem a little fuzzy if you're using an older iPhone.)

- If you're on a FaceTime conversation and the Grid button isn't available, press the screen to toggle it on and off.
- Tap the button one more to disable the grid.

SHARE YOUR SCREEN IN FACETIME CALL ON IPHONE

Sharing your screen from the FaceTime app (on a device that fulfills the minimal system requirements) allows you to include other software into a call. You may share a picture album, seek comments on a project, and more while everyone on the call can see and hear your responses.

Cast your desktop during a FaceTime chat

If the FaceTime controls aren't already visible while you're on a call, press the screen to reveal them, and then tap the Share Content option.

- Share your whole display by selecting the Share My Screen option.

The Share Content button will display a countdown from three to one before sending a thumbnail of your screen to the recipient of your FaceTime conversation. Call participants may touch to expand the image and read your message.

The Share Content option allows you to start or stop screen sharing.

COLLABORATE ON PROJECTS WITH MESSAGES ON IPHONE

The Messages app makes it easy to invite contacts to work together on a project by adding them to a shared document, spreadsheet, or other file.

Please note that in order to begin working on a project with others through Messages, all participants must be using iMessage on iOS 16, iPadOS 16, or macOS 13 or later, and the material must be saved in a shared location such as iCloud Drive. If you want to utilize the in-app collaboration capabilities of an iPhone app, you may need to enable iCloud. To do so, go to Settings > [your name] > iCloud > Show All (below Apps Using iCloud).

Solicit participation in a joint effort

Messages may be used as a discussion forum for material created in other apps that you ask others to work on together. You may collaborate with others on information created in Notes, Freeform, Reminders, Safari, Keynote, Numbers, and Pages, and more by enabling the sharing option in iCloud settings and storing the work in a shared location like iCloud Drive.

How you go about asking someone to work together is app specific. One possible method of initiating a group project in one of these apps is as follows:

To send a file to a collaborator, first choose it and then either hit the Share button or the Collaborate button.

To work together, choose Collaborate (instead of Send Copy) and then hit the desired contacts. Tap the Messages app icon if you don't see the group or individual mentioned.

The recommended symbols might represent people or groups currently engaged in a FaceTime session or recent Messages exchange.

The invitation is already composed and ready to send when a Messages chat begins. Then, write a quick letter and hit the Send button.

Notes drawing invitation demonstrating Collaborate sharing option and "Only people you invite can edit" access and authorization setting for collaborative drawing creation. Below that is a list of four potential receivers, one of which is an organization. Sharing options, including AirDrop, Messages, Mail, and Freeform, are shown on the bottom row.

After inviting people in Messages, you may go to the other app to work on the project and then come back to the chat in Messages by hitting the Collaborate icon.

Changes to the file are highlighted in the Messages thread's top post. To see the latest modifications to the collaborative project, just choose an update.

Before others may see changes or engage with your shared item, they may need to accept your invitation or join the shared item.

Use Messages to coordinate on a task.

When you invite others to work on a project, the dialogue in Messages will automatically update to reflect any changes made.

- Launch the iPhone's Messages application.
- To go back to the project you were working on when you received the invitation, open the thread containing the invite.
- To see the attachment in chat, tap on it.
- When an update appears at the top of the thread, choose it by tapping Show.
- Select the person or group's name at the top of the page, then select Collaboration and finally the shared project.

Any time you make a modification to the project, everyone involved will be notified in the thread.

It's important to remember that inviting someone to join a group chat means inviting them to participate in the projects you're working on together. A notice will appear at the top of the screen if they have recently been joined to the group chat. Or you might ask them to work together.

Keep everyone on the same page and in sync.

It's possible that the persons working on the file aren't the same as those in the Messages cooperation. You may invite folks to work on the file with you in a space other than Messages. Alternatively, you might have two distinct teams in Messages, each carrying on its own collaboration thread.

In a group Messages chat, you and your collaborators may easily add and delete members as needed.

- Launch the iPhone's Messages application.
- To see information about a group discussion, enter the chat you want to moderate and click the group symbol at the chat's top.
- Select the chat participants by tapping the corresponding button.
- Include further people: To add contacts, go to the bottom of the list and touch Add Contact.

If you and another person began working together but later decided to bring in other individuals, you'll need to start a new dialogue.

Please remember that any previously shared files in the chat must be made available to new participants. A notice will show at the top of the chat when new people are added. To see the files that have already been shared and to which you may invite additional people, tap Show in the notice.

Take people out of the discussion: To delete a contact, swipe left on their name and then hit the Delete button.

It's crucial to remember that the applications used for collaboration often handle project access management. Participant access may be managed inside the app itself, so you can take away their ability to see or make changes at any time.

You may choose to include the new person in the current discussion about the paper, or you can start a new one if you like. New discussion participants won't see old messages from before they were added.

Messages is where you may break off project collaboration.

Typically, a project's access is managed by the app where the collaboration takes place. In the case of document collaboration in Pages, for instance, the app's own settings will take priority over those in Messages. However, like every other message in the chat, the invitation may be unsent or deleted.

Note that removing an invitation from a thread does not remove people from the file, just the discussion it was linked with. Verify user permissions inside the app to permanently disable access to any content.

SHARE CONTENT IN MESSAGES ON IPHONE

The Messages app allows you to send and receive text, photos, and links. A Shared with You tab will appear in the appropriate applications if someone sends you material. Shared with You is supported by a wide variety of media and information apps.

Give people access to your material

- Launch the iPhone's Messages application.
- Initiate a brand-new discussion or message.
- Pick one of these options:
- Insert a picture or a link by copying and pasting it into your post.
- Select Photos from the list of apps, then select to upload a photo or video from your recent captures.
- To send an attachment to a contact or the Messages app, press the attachment, then the Share button.
- In addition to sending your file, you may copy it, save it, or print it by clicking the Share option.
- Type in a note, and then hit the Send button.

- Select the item you'd want to send to Messages from inside another app (such as Podcasts, News, or Music), press the More icon, then hit Share.

Look up anything that was sent to you by a certain person.

- Launch the iPhone's Messages application.
- Start the discussion whose results you want.
- To begin a chat with a specific individual or group, tap their name.
- To see what has been shared with you, please scroll down.

Please take note that if the sender is not in your contacts, the content will not display in the Shared with "You" section.

Photos, Safari, News, Music, and Podcasts are just few of the applications that have a Shared with You tab.

Preview and download media.

Collages consist of two or three objects, while stacks consist of four or more if you get many photographs or movies at once.

➢ Launch the iPhone's Messages application.

- ➢ Pick one of these options:
  - Take a peek inside a pile: To see, respond to, or engage with each individual picture or video in a stack, tap to open, then swipe left or right.
  - To save an image or video: Select the Save Photo option after selecting several images.

Tie together information that other people have shared

You can easily "pin" material that someone shares in Messages, making it stand out in the Shared with You area of compatible applications, in Messages search, and in the conversation details (the information you see when you press the name at the top of the chat).

- Launch the iPhone's Messages application.
- Start the discussion off with the material you want to bookmark.
- Pin the link by touching and holding the message bubble that contains it.

Keep in mind that you may add images to your collection, but you can't pin them.

Cover up your tracks

- You may disable the Shared with You section in an app's settings.
- Navigate to the Shared with You section of the Settings menu.
- Disable Shared with You for a particular app or Automatic Sharing.

HAVE A GROUP CONVERSATION IN MESSAGES ON IPHONE

Send a group text message using the Messages app. You may bring up particular messages and work on a project together in a group chat.

Initiate a brand-new group chat.

A group chat may be initiated by sending a single message to many recipients.

- Launch the iPhone's Messages application.
- Start a new chat by tapping the Compose button.
- To add recipients, either type in their phone numbers, click the Add Contact option, then choose contacts, or use their Apple IDs.

Please take note that your message bubbles will be green instead of blue if any of your receivers are not utilizing iMessage.

- Select the message box, press the keyboard, and then select the Send option.

Join an ongoing discussion with another person.

Additional contacts may be added to a group chat if there are already at least two participants. If not, you'll need to initiate a fresh round of small talk.

- Launch the iPhone's Messages application.
- Select the chat in which you'd want to invite a new member.
- To see how many people are participating in the chat, touch the group name at the top of the screen.
- Choose "Add Contact," then add the recipient's number, name, or Apple ID.
- Select a contact from your list, or add a new one by tapping the Add Contact button.
- Follow the on-screen prompts to create a new group if any members of the existing group have not enabled iMessage.
- Swipe left on a person's name in a group chat, then hit Remove to kick them out.

Get out of a discussion

- Launch the iPhone's Messages application.

- Select the chat you want to exit by tapping on it.
- Select the chat group by tapping its name at the top.
- Please scroll down and press Cut off or delete and block this person from further contact.
- Blocked chats are archived in the Recently Deleted section and may be accessed there if necessary. Find out how to delete and ban certain chats.

Conversation notifications may be disabled as well.

Introduce individuals into a discussion.

Individual members of a group chat will be alerted when they are specifically mentioned in a message. Even if the individual you mention has the discussion muted, they may still get a notification depending on their settings.

- Launch the iPhone's Messages application.
- Type the first few letters of a contact's name to initiate a discussion with them.
- When the name of a contact pops up, tap on it.
- In Messages, you may also send a message to a specific person by entering @ followed by that person's name.

- Go to Settings > Messages > Notify Me to customize how you're alerted when you're referenced in a conversation.

Transform a group chat into a different name and picture.

You may give a group discussion a name and then choose an appropriate picture to symbolize it. The new identity will be visible to anybody using iMessage.

- Launch the iPhone's Messages application.
- To begin a new discussion, tap the person's name or phone number.
- Select an item under Change Name and Photo and tap Done.

USE VIDEO CONFERENCING FEATURES ON IPHONE

Full-screen video effects and the ability to respond with hand gestures that fill the camera frame with 3D effects are available during a FaceTime chat or a call made with any third-party video conferencing software.

Include visual effects on your next video call.

- Launch Control Center when participating in a Face Time or third-party video conferencing conversation.
- Select a Video Effect from the menu that appears.

In a portrait mode, the backdrop is subtly blurred and the attention is placed squarely on the subject. To change how much the backdrop is blurred, tap the More Controls icon. See Include visual effects on your next video call.

Studio lighting is designed to isolate your face from the backdrop. The studio light may be dimmed by tapping the More Controls icon.

Allows you to add responses using hand gestures. Although adding responses using hand gestures is disabled when responses is off in Control Center, you may still do so by touching the icons that display when you touch and hold your tile during a conversation.

The FaceTime call's Control Center video effects options. By activating Portrait mode, the caller's photograph is shown in an expanded tile with a blurred backdrop and a centered topic.

The FaceTime app (and other video conferencing applications) allows users to add responses with simple hand movements that fill the camera frame with enjoyable 3D augmented reality effects like hearts, balloons, fireworks, and more.

To include these responses, touch and hold your tile throughout the call, then press the corresponding icons.

In order to employ hand gestures, click Control Center, choose Video Effects, and toggle on Reactions. Keep your hands out of your face and wait a second or two for the motion to take effect.

USE SHAREPLAY TO WATCH, LISTEN AND PLAY TOGETHER IN FACETIME ON IPHONE

The SharePlay feature in the FaceTime app allows you to watch or listen to the same media while on a FaceTime chat with friends or family. With shared controls and synchronized playback, everyone on the call can experience the same moments at the same time. Using smart volume, you may keep a conversation going while viewing or listening to media. In addition to chatting with pals using FaceTime, you may play supported multiplayer games together in Game Center.

Holding two iPhones together automatically initiates SharePlay.

- To begin a SharePlay session, bring two iPhones together and follow the instructions there.

During a FaceTime chat, you may utilize SharePlay in any app you choose. Select the applications for SharePlay option from the Share Content menu during a call to see which applications may be used for SharePlay.

Some SharePlay-enabled applications may need a paid membership. Each viewer must have a subscription to, or have purchased, the material on their own device, and each device must fulfill the minimum system requirements in order to see the movie or TV program together. Some movies and TV series may not be compatible with SharePlay because of regional restrictions. It's possible that certain nations and areas don't have access to FaceTime or some FaceTime capabilities, as well as other Apple services.

View a shared video while on a FaceTime chat.

FaceTime calls allow you to view videos with your loved ones while keeping everyone in sync.

Playback controls are located on top of the video, while a tiny window displaying the content's sharer occupies the remainder of the screen.

- Launch the iPhone's FaceTime app and initiate a call.
- Select an app from the drop-down menu and then hit the Share button. Shared listening and gaming (through, say, an Apple TV app)
- Alternatively, you may access a SharePlay-compatible video streaming app directly from the Home Screen.
- To start viewing a program or movie with everyone on the call, choose the one you want to watch, hit the Play button, and then choose Play for Everyone (if the option displays). (The other call participants may need to choose Join SharePlay in order to see the video.)

The video begins playing simultaneously for everyone on the call who can see it. Users who aren't already subscribed, purchased, or using a free trial period are encouraged to do so.

Each viewer has their own set of playback controls that allow them to start, stop, rewind, and fast-forward the program. Every user has their own independent settings (such as closed captioning and loudness).

If you don't want to pause a movie or TV show to check your email or make a phone call, you can utilize Picture in Picture to continue viewing the video while switching to another app.

During a FaceTime conversation, you and a buddy may view a video from a compatible app.

When using the Apple TV app (or any compatible video app) on an iPhone with the minimal system requirements, you may initiate a FaceTime call while browsing or viewing video content, and then share it in sync with others via SharePlay. All participants must have paid or free access to the material on their own devices at the same time.

Find the video you wish to share in the Apple TV app (or another compatible video app), then touch it to see its information.

- Select Share, and then select SharePlay.

- Enter the names of the people you wish to share with in the To box, and then choose FaceTime.
- To begin utilizing SharePlay when a FaceTime call has been established, choose Start or Play.

Recipients may then press Open to begin watching.

Anyone who isn't already a subscriber may do so in advance of seeing any material that needs membership.

The video may be streamed to Apple TV once it has begun playing. See SharePlay content may be sent to Apple TV.

SharePlay content may be sent to Apple TV.

You may continue viewing a video with a group on the large screen by sending it from an iPhone to Apple TV.

To do one of the following on an iPhone:

- To play content on an Apple TV, open the app and choose AirPlay from the menu.

- To choose Apple TV as the media player, launch Control Center and hit the Playback Destination button.

On Apple TV, the video will play in sync, and you can continue the discussion on your iPhone.

Share some tunes during a FaceTime chat.

During a FaceTime chat, you and your friends may listen to a shared album or playlist. Participants may listen in, see what's next, contribute songs to a shared queue, and more so long as they have access to the music (for example, via a subscription, a transaction, or a free trial) on a device that matches the minimal system requirements.

An example of a SharePlay session in action during a FaceTime chat, complete with synchronized playback of Apple Music tracks. At the top of the screen, you'll see the face of the person sharing the material; below the FaceTime controls, you'll see the album picture; and above the album image, you'll see the playing controls.

- Launch a FaceTime conference call.
- Select a music streaming service from the list and then click the Share option. Shared

listening and gaming (through, say, an Apple TV app)

- Alternatively, you may access the SharePlay-compatible music streaming app directly from the Home screen itself (the Music app, for instance).

To start listening to music together, first choose the songs you wish to hear and then press the Play button. (The other call participants may need to choose Join SharePlay in order to hear the music.)

Everyone on the call who can hear the music will hear it simultaneously. Users who aren't already subscribed, purchased, or using a free trial period are encouraged to do so.

Each listener has access to their own set of buttons for pausing, rewinding, speeding up, skipping forward, and selecting a new song. Additionally, everyone on the call may contribute to the playlist.

During a FaceTime conversation, you may invite your pals to listen to music from a compatible app.

Starting a FaceTime conversation in the Music app (or other compatible music app) on an iPhone with the minimal system requirements allows you to utilize SharePlay to share the music in sync with others on the call. Each listener has their own set of buttons for pausing, rewinding, speeding up, and skipping around the song. In addition, any SharePlay user may contribute music to the group's collective playlist. The individuals you wish to send it to must also have access to the music (via a subscription, for instance).

Launch Apple Music (or another compatible music app) and choose the track(s) you want to share.

Pick one of the options below:

- To share the music, open the menu by tapping the More icon and choosing SharePlay.
- Select "More" from the menu bar, then "Share" and finally "SharePlay."
- Enter the names of the people you wish to share with in the To box, and then choose FaceTime.
- Tap the Start button once the FaceTime call has connected.

Recipients may begin playing by tapping the song's title in the FaceTime interface's header, followed by tapping Open to begin playing. Those that have access to the material on the call will hear the music begin simultaneously.

Users who do not have permission to see the material you are sharing will be prompted to request permission.

During a FaceTime chat, you and your pals may play games from Game Center.

FaceTime calls may be used to play supported multiplayer games in Game Center with pals. You'll need to create a Game Center account in Settings, add friends, and then search the App Store for a multi-player game that supports Game Center before you can play it.

- Open the game during a FaceTime chat, then hit Start SharePlay and proceed with the on-screen prompts.

CHANGE FACETIME VIDEO SETTINGS ON IPHONE

When on a FaceTime conversation, you have the option to disable the camera, switch between cameras, or use Portrait mode.

Portrait mode allows you to blur the backdrop.

Similar to the Camera app's Portrait mode, Portrait mode may be activated on compatible devices to automatically blur the backdrop and center the camera's view on the subject.

- Tap the tile while you're on a FaceTime call.
- To blur the tile's background, choose the appropriate button.
- You may cancel Portrait mode by tapping the button again.

Control Center also allows you to activate Portrait mode. Launch the Settings app and choose the Video Effects tab.

Change to the back camera

- To switch to the rear camera during a FaceTime chat, press your tile and then the corresponding button.
- You may reverse the process by tapping the Flip to Back Camera button again.
- To see more detail while utilizing the back camera, just touch the 1x button. If you tap it again, the picture will be restored to its original size.

Put away the camera

- To turn on the camera during a FaceTime chat, just touch the screen to see the call controls. (Re-tapping it will activate the camera once again.)

CHANGE FACETIME AUDIO SETTINGS ON IPHONE

With the FaceTime app and its spatial audio capabilities, it will seem as if your pals are right there with you. Their voices are dispersed and seem to originate from where each character is physically located on the screen.

Please take note that AirPods (3rd generation), AirPods Pro (all models), and AirPods Max (each sold separately) are compatible with Spatial Audio.

Silence the ambient noise

Turn on Voice Isolation mode (on compatible models) if you want just your voice to be heard during a FaceTime chat. During a FaceTime conversation, you may isolate your voice using the Voice Isolation setting.

- Launch the Settings menu while on a FaceTime chat, then hit Mic Mode and finally choose Voice Isolation.

- Standard, Voice Isolation, and Wide Spectrum are shown in the Control Center Mic Mode options for FaceTime conversations.

Take into account the ambient noise

- Wide Spectrum mode (on compatible devices) allows you to hear both your speech and the ambient noise during a FaceTime chat.
- To use Wide Spectrum while on a FaceTime chat, open the Control Center, hit Mic Mode, and then pick it.

Silence the noise

- To silence a FaceTime call, press the screen to bring up the FaceTime menu (if it isn't already showing), then hit the Mute Off button.
- You may press the button again to restore normal playback.
- When the volume drops, your microphone will pick up your voice and alert you to the fact that your mic is muted; to unmute it, just hit the Mute On button.

CHAPTER EIGHT

HOW TO NAVIGATE THE PHOTOS APP ON IPHONE

The Photos app on the iPhone and iPad includes several useful options for cataloging and storing your photos and videos. Images may be instantly viewed by day, month, or year, and the location where each was taken can be quickly verified. Finding a photo from a recent vacation to display on your digital picture frame is now simpler than before.

HOW TO SWITCH YEARS, MONTHS, AND DAYS IN THE IPHONE AND IPAD PHOTOS APP

Get started with Photos on your iOS device.

If you aren't currently in the Library, tap the tab in the far left corner of the screen.

Methods for Changing Dates and Years

- Choose the timeline view that interests you by tapping Years, Months, Days, or All Photos.
- Starting at Years, tapping on a certain year will reveal the Months underneath.

- To switch to Days view from Months, just touch on the desired month.
- If you click on a picture, you'll get a slideshow of every photo taken that day.

Above the photo galleries' tabs is a navigation bar where you may exit your current view by selecting Years, Months, or Days.

To go back a level, just swipe left from the edge of your screen. However, this motion won't function when viewing photographs individually. Swiping just advances to the previous or next picture, so you'll need to use the back button in the upper left corner instead.

How to See Where Photos and Videos Were Taken on a Map

- Open the Camera app on your iOS device.
- Make sure you're in the Library section, where you can easily navigate between Years, Months, Days, and All Photos.
- To see your photos by month or day, open Photos.
- Select the collection you want to edit by tapping the "..." button that appears on the thumbnail in either the Months or Days display.

- Pick the option to display the map.
- Select Show Map from the Menu.

The locations of the images for that day or month will shown on a map. Keep in mind that the Camera app cannot capture the geolocation data unless Location Services are enabled. There will be no retroactive effect of this.

HOW TO SELECT A MONTH IN THE YEARS VIEW AND JUMP TO IT INSTANTLY

- Unlike in earlier versions of iOS, iOS 14 does not allow you to browse a whole year's worth of images at once. In its place is a tile for each year that cycles through pictures from that year's months. If you touch the year tile, you'll be sent directly to the month view for the current picture. By utilizing the scrubbing motion, you may go forward one month.
- Open the Camera app on your iOS device.
- You need to be in the Library section, which is subdivided into Years, Months, and Days.
- In Photos, choose the Years tab.
- Open Camera, then click the Years option in the Photos menu.
- Look for the year you're interested in.

- Slide your finger over the tile in a horizontal motion.

The month should show beneath the year, and the thumbnail image on the tile will update as you go through the months.

- If you tap the collection's name, you'll be sent directly to the month you were last scouring.
- By swiping your finger left and right over the Years tile, you may quickly move between the months.

TIPS FOR IMMEDIATELY ADDING MOMENTS IMAGES AND VIDEOS TO THE CLIPBOARD

- Open the Camera app on your iOS device.
- If you haven't already, go to the Library section.
- In the All Photos section, you may search for the media files you want to publish.
- Click the Select button on the far right.
- To choose a picture, start Photos, go to All Photos, and then click Select.
- Select several photographs or videos at once by tapping on them or by dragging your finger over multiple rows or columns.

- To share, just click the button. That's the square symbol in the lower left corner of your screen with the arrow going upward.
- Choose "Copy Photos" from the menu that appears.
- Choose an item from your gallery, then go to the Share menu and choose Copy Photos.

You may now copy your media files to the clipboard and paste them into an email or document that supports media. If you just want to copy a single photo or clip, you may do it by holding down on it until a context menu appears. Finally, choose the Copy option.

USE MARKUP ON YOUR IPHONE

Markup allows you to make changes to screenshots and photographs, alter the opacity and thickness of fonts, and even sign a PDF.

Markup-based software and functionalities

The following are some examples of Markup-compatible software and how to get started with them:

Mail

To create a new email, launch Mail and choose the write option. or answer an already existing email.

Select the text you want to format, then either touch the gray arrow icon or press Return. press the email's body, then press the ellipsis button next to it, then choose Insert Media. The arrow button may be used to navigate the list of choices.

To attach and annotate a picture or PDF, choose the Camera or Document button and go to its location.

Select the attachment, and then the arrow button. Mark up your document by clicking the Markup button. To include a signature, text, and more, just tap the + button.

To send your message, tap Done.

Messages

To begin a new discussion, launch Messages and choose Compose from the menu. Or you could join a current discussion.

- Select an image by tapping the Photos icon.

To annotate an attached picture, touch the photo and choose Markup. You may now draw on the picture, or use the + button to get other Markup tools.

- Do a Save, then a Done.
- Choose the Send option.

Photos

- Select the image you want by clicking on Photos.
- To add a note, go to Edit and then Markup. To insert text, shapes, and other elements, click the Add button.
- Use the "Done" button twice.

Use Markup to Draw

Select a Markup tool (pen, highlighter, pencil) and a color before beginning to draw. You may adjust the transparency of colors by using the same tool again, or you can adjust the thickness by tapping a different tool. To adjust the color saturation, choose the Color option.

Transpose a sketch

You're free to reposition your creation once you've drawn it. Select the Lasso tool by pressing the button, then draw a circle around the object you wish to relocate and drop it.

Cancelling a drawing's changes

To start again with a drawing, choose the eraser tool by double-tapping the paper's eraser icon. The Undo button allows you to undo your most recent markup operation. If you shake your smartphone and then hit Redo, all undone markings will be restored.

- Type your name, insert a magnifier, and customize the forms.
- Click the Add button to get further Markup options:
- To change the text color, press the circle; to change the font, size, and alignment, hit the formatting button.

Create or append a signature to a document quickly.

Move the loupe anywhere you'd want it to go, scale it up or down with the blue dot, and tweak the magnification with the green dot.

To include a shape in a screenshot, picture, or PDF, just tap it. Position the form where you'd want it, then tweak its dimensions and orientation using the blue dots. The arc of the arrow and the shape of the bubble may be customized using the green dots.

HOW TO USE MARKUP TO WRITE OR DRAW PHOTOS ON MAC

Markup allows you to annotate a picture by adding text, shapes, cropping, rotating, and more.

Please be aware that the Markup tools cannot be used to edit a video.

- To edit an image in Photos, double-click it and choose Edit from the menu bar.
- Markup may be added by clicking the Extensions icon.
- Mark up the picture with the aid of the icons provided in the toolbar.
- Place the cursor towards the margins of the markup you want to modify, and then drag the blue handles.
- Put your changes into effect by selecting Save.
- Select the image you want to edit, then go to Edit > Extensions > Markup.
- ✓ Tool
- ✓ Description
- ✓ Sketch

Create a form by drawing a single line.

If the form you drew is one of the predefined ones, it will be substituted for it; if you want to use your own shape instead, choose it from the palette that appears.

Draw

Make a form using only one line. By applying additional pressure to the trackpad, you may make the line you're drawing thicker and darker.

Force Touch trackpads are required for this feature to appear.

Shapes

You may reposition the shapes by clicking and dragging them. Adjust the size of the form by dragging its blue handles. You may change its form by manipulating its green handles, if present.

Highlight

To highlight shapes, first select them by clicking the Shapes button. Move the spotlight to the desired location. Adjust the size using the blue resizing handles.

Enlarge

Select the desired shape and then use the Loupe button. To zoom in on a certain region, just move the loupe there. The magnification may be adjusted by dragging the green handle, and the loupe's size can be altered by dragging the blue handle. A series of loupes may be superimposed on a picture to enlarge certain details.

Make a second loupe by holding the Option key while dragging an existing one, then place it on top of the first and modify its location using the alignment instructions to see details more clearly.

Text

After entering your content, you may reposition the text area.

- ❖ Featured Picks
- ❖ Underline the chosen passages.
- ❖ Types of Lines
- ❖ Modify a shape's line thickness, line type, and shadow.
- ❖ Edge Style
- ❖ Alter the line color to make a form stand out.
- ❖ Input Color
- ❖ Modify the fill color of a shape.
- ❖ Format of Text

Alter the typeface or font color and style.

- Flip to the left or flip to the right
- Select the leftward rotation option by clicking the Rotate Left button. Keep clicking to keep the wheel turning.

- Hold the Option key down while clicking the Rotate Right tool to rotate an object to the right.

Crop

Cover up an imperfection. Pull the corner handles to isolate the specific region you want to preserve inside the frame. The picture frame may be dragged to a new location. To begin cropping, choose the option.

A place to add, read, and alter picture descriptions. (When a picture includes a description, the tool becomes visible.)

Image descriptions are helpful for those who have trouble seeing images on the web because they can be read aloud by screen readers. For instance, the VoiceOver command VO-Shift-L may be used with the Mac's built-in screen reader VoiceOver to hear a description of the picture that the VoiceOver cursor is hovering over. See the VoiceOver User Guide for additional information about using VoiceOver.

Make notes on

Use your nearest iOS device to make notes by drawing or sketching on a document. To annotate on one of your devices, use the Annotate button when the other is close. Once your gadget is linked, a highlight might appear on the tool. You may stop the tool from working by clicking it again.

HOW TO DELETE PHOTOS ON YOUR IPHONE

You may choose to remove only one picture or many at once. If you remove anything by mistake, don't worry; you can get it back.

A word of caution before you hit that delete

The images and movies you care about should be backed up regularly. For photos and videos stored in iCloud, when you delete them from one device, they are also removed from all others where you have logged in with the same Apple ID. Figure out why and how you can remove media from iCloud Photos.

- Go to Settings > General > [Device] Storage to see your available storage space. Find out how to better handle the pictures on your mobile device.

Getting rid of media

Photos and movies that have been deleted are stored in the Recently Deleted album for 30 days. They will be erased forever when the 30-day period has passed.

When you utilize iCloud photographs, any photographs or videos you delete from one device will also be removed from all other devices.

Photos that were transferred to your iPhone or iPad from a computer cannot be deleted through the Photos app on the device itself. When trying to remove a picture from an iPhone or iPad, if the Trash button is gray, you may need to cease syncing photographs from your computer. Find out how to disable automatic picture synchronization on your PC.

iPhone instructions for erasing a single picture Choice to Delete Images

- View the images.
- To remove a picture or video, go to the Library menu, then hit All Photos.
- Select Delete Photo by clicking the Trash icon.

Methods for Removing Numerous Pictures

- Multiple images from the Photos app on an iPhone.
- View the images.
- Select All Photos from the Library menu.
- Select numerous images by tapping or swiping your finger over the thumbnails.

- Select the trash can icon and then confirm your deletions.

Create an iCloud Shared Photo Library on iOS 16.1, iPadOS 16.1, or later, and share your photos with up to five people at once. The materials in the Shared Library may be removed, added to, or altered by any user. You will no longer be able to view media that has been removed from the Shared Library by another user. The original uploader is the only one who may remove or restore a file from the Recently Deleted folder of the Shared Library. If you want to restore an item from your Recently Deleted album, you have 30 days to do so.

The removal of redundant media

- Select Albums from the Photos menu.
- Select Utilities, then the Duplicates album.
- Select Merge to merge all identical items.
- To confirm, tap Merge [Count] Items.

When you merge images on your phone, it takes the two and chooses the one with the greatest quality and most information to save. All of the other copies will be found in the "Recently Deleted" album.

The Duplicates album is compatible with iOS 16 and later, namely iPadOS 16.1. The process of finding duplicates is automated but might take some time.

Retrieve lost video or stills

- To see albums, launch Photos.
- Select Utilities, then the Most Recently Deleted album.

You may use Face ID or Touch ID to access your Recently Deleted album with iOS 16 and later, along with iPadOS 16.1 and later.

- Select by tapping it.
- Choose the media file you want to retrieve and then press Recover. Select Recover All to retrieve all of the media from the album.
- To confirm, click the Recover Photo button.

You have 30 days to retrieve deleted media from the Recently Deleted album after making an inadvertent deletion. Photos and movies that have been recovered are added to your Library.

You should enable access to the Recently Deleted album by default.

- Accessed the Settings menu.
- Select Images.

Put an end to using Face ID.

The Hidden and Recently Deleted albums are protected in iOS 16 and later by default and may only be accessed with Face ID or Touch ID. Turning off Use Face ID will also automatically unlock the Hidden album. Figure up a way to conceal your pictures.

- Get rid of pictures for good
- To see albums, launch Photos.
- Select the album that was just removed.

You may use Face ID or Touch ID to access your Recently Deleted album with iOS 16 and later, along with iPadOS 16.1 and later.

- Select by tapping it.
- Tap the Delete button after selecting the desired image or clip. Select Delete All to get rid of everything in the album at once.
- Select the Delete Photo button to confirm.
- A removed picture from this album cannot be recovered.

CHAPTER NINE

EDIT PHOTOS AND VIDEOS ON IPHONE

Use the iPhone's Photos app to modify your photos and videos after taking them. You may play about with the exposure and color, as well as cut, rotate, and apply filters. If you decide you don't like your edits, you may undo them by tapping the Cancel button.

Any changes you make to your photographs and movies in iCloud photographs will be reflected on all of your devices.

Adapt the hue and brightness.

You may expand any thumbnail image in Photos to its full resolution by tapping on it.

- To access the picture effects including Exposure, Brilliance, Highlights, and Shadows, tap Edit and then slide left beneath the image.
- Select the effect you want to modify, then fine-tune it by dragging the slider.

You can quickly see which effects have been amplified or muted by looking at the degree to which their individual buttons are shaded. You may compare the modified effect to the unmodified one by tapping the effect button.

Editing a snapshot in the middle of the screen. The photo's brightness was adjusted using the slider located underneath the image. The Brightness slider is located underneath the editing tools. To the right of the slider are the options to Adjust, apply a filter, or crop the image. It's set to adjust by default. There is a Cancel button in the upper left corner and a Finish button in the upper right. The Undo, Redo, Adjust, Markup, and Plug-ins buttons are also located at the top of the screen.

If you're happy with your modifications, press Done; otherwise, hit Cancel and then Discard modifications.

Use the Enhance button to instantly apply filters to your photographs and videos.

Trim, spin, or invert a video or image

You may expand any thumbnail image in Photos to its full resolution by tapping on it.

- Select Crop by selecting the Edit menu, then doing one of the following:
- Use the manual cropping tools by dragging the rectangle's edges to include just the part of the image you wish to preserve, or by pinching the image to choose a smaller or larger region.
- Scale down to a uniform aspect ratio: Click the Aspect Ratio Freeform button, and then choose a desired aspect ratio from the drop-down menu that appears.
- The picture may be rotated 90 degrees with a tap of the Rotate button.
- To horizontally flip a picture, just choose the Flip option.

The Adjust, Filters, and Crop controls are located at the very bottom of the display, going from left to right. The Crop option is chosen, and a slider is used to fine-tune the geometric improvements. There is a Cancel button in the upper left corner and a Finish button in the upper right. The Flip, Auto, Aspect Ratio, Markup, and Plug-ins buttons are also located at the top of the screen, going from left to right.

If you're happy with your modifications, press Done; otherwise, hit Cancel and then Discard modifications.

Pinch the image to zoom in and crop it fast while viewing it. When the image is positioned as you'd want it cropped, choose Crop from the menu in the screen's upper right. To finalize your cropping, click the Done button.

Shift your focus and readjust your viewpoint

You may expand any thumbnail image in Photos to its full resolution by tapping on it.

- Select Crop from the Edit menu.
- To access the retouching options, such as Straighten, Vertical, and Horizontal, swipe left beneath the image.
- Select the effect you want to modify, then fine-tune it by dragging the slider.

By looking at the outline surrounding each button, you can see at a glance which effects have been scaled up or down according to your preferences. You may switch between the original and the modified effect with a tap of the button.

If you're happy with your modifications, press Done; otherwise, hit Cancel and then Discard modifications.

Utilize modifying filters

You may expand any thumbnail image in Photos to its full resolution by tapping on it.

- o Filter effects like Vivid and Dramatic may be applied by selecting Edit and then Filters.
- o Applying Original will undo the effects of any filters that were active at the time of capture.

Editing a snapshot in the middle of the screen. The Adjust, Filters, and Crop controls are located at the very bottom of the display, going from left to right. Selecting the Filters menu brings up a control slider for adjusting the filter's strength. There is a Cancel button in the upper left corner and a Finish button in the upper right. The Undo, Redo, Filters, Markup, and Plug-ins buttons are also located at the top of the display, moving from left to right.

- o To modify the intensity of a filter's effect, tap it and move the slider.
- o Tap the image to see how it was altered in comparison to the original.
- o If you're happy with your modifications, press Done; otherwise, hit Cancel and then Discard modifications.

Reverting changes

You may undo or redo several edits by tapping the corresponding buttons at the top of the screen while you work on a picture or video.

- To see the difference between the original and the finalized version of a picture or video, just touch on it.
- Change many images at once by copying and pasting your changes
- A picture's (or a video's) modifications may be copied and pasted into another photo or many photographs simultaneously.
- Launch the media file that already has the changes you wish to replicate.
- Click the More menu, then choose Copy Edits.
- Use the back button to go back to your reading list.
- Select the photographs you wish to apply the changes to by tapping on their thumbnails. Or, launch a standalone image or clip.
- Select Paste Edits by clicking the More button.

To ensure a perfect fit, Photos automatically adjusts the white balance and exposure of each picture to make them seem as identical as possible.

Undo the changes to a video or picture

You may undo your changes to an edited picture or video at any time after you've saved it.

To see more editing choices for a picture or video, open it.

Go back to the original version by selecting it.

- Modify the time and place
- Metadata information in a picture or video may be edited to reflect a new creation date, time, or place. See View related images and videos.
- Launch the media file and hit the "More" button.
- Try modifying the time and date or moving the map around.
- After making the necessary changes, click the Adjust button.
- Select, select the thumbnails you wish to edit, and then follow the instructions above to adjust the date, time, and location of many photographs at once.

Photos and videos may be reset to their original time and place of capture. You may undo your changes by tapping the More button, then Adjust Date & Time or Adjust Location, and finally Revert.

Put your mark on a picture.

Photos allows you to expand any image by tapping on it.

- Select Mark Up from the Edit menu.
- Use the various pens, markers, and fills to add your own commentary to the picture. You may use the magnifier, a description, some text, some shapes, or even your signature by using the Add Annotations button.

If you're happy with your modifications, press Done to save them; otherwise, hit Cancel to discard them.

HOW TO EASILY REMOVE OBJECTS FROM YOUR PICTURES

Enhance your pictures by manipulating the

You've undoubtedly been in this situation: you're enjoying a beautiful shot you took when you notice something ugly in the background. Perhaps there are stray power wires in your #foodphoto or a few crumbs of bread in an otherwise beautiful photograph.

You don't have to be a pro at picture editing to use TouchRetouch to get rid of these pesky items. This miraculous tool employs sophisticated algorithms to eliminate them instantly and invisibly.

When you open TouchRetouch and choose a picture for editing, a set of tools will appear at the program's bottom. Take a short look at their functioning here.

The Quick Fix feature is the simplest to use. In the above picture, the dog toy and electrical outlet have both been eliminated.

To begin, choose the desired tool by tapping it and then swiping over the unwanted element, as if you were painting over it. While you're at it, a magnified view will pop up in the corner to assist you get in the nitty-gritty. However, precision is not necessary. TouchRetouch is intelligent enough to complete the form automatically. Overpaint rather than underpaint if you must.

TouchRetouch is activated when you remove your finger from the screen. Just as in the video, it's that simple!

Removing Items: Sweep up the Crumbs

Precision is often required when dealing with difficult materials or intricate designs. The Object Removal feature is useful for this same purpose. The crumbs in the photo of the coffee on the textured mat were digitally removed using Object Removal.

The first step is to "paint" over the damaged area with your finger, much as in Quick Repair. However, now you may make several strokes, customize brush size through the Settings button, and use the eraser tool to undo any mistakes. When you're ready, press the Go button.

Do away with the power wires!

Power lines are a common photographic nuisance that are easy to overlook. The Line Removal tool, thankfully, makes it a breeze.

Simply tap the tool and draw anywhere close to the power line to use it. TouchRetouch will automatically zap the whole power line to make sure it is completely straight, so there's no need to worry if your line isn't exactly straight.

USE MEMORIES IN PHOTOS ON YOUR IPHONE

The Photos app can identify special people, locations, and moments in your collection and organize them into themed albums called Memories. You may even make your own Memories and show them off to your loved ones.

Verify that you are running the most recent version of iOS or iPadOS on your iPhone, iPad, or iPod touch.

Make sure you're logged into iCloud on all of your devices using the same Apple ID, then activate iCloud Photos, and your memories will be synced automatically.

Think Back on the Past

- Launch Camera Roll and choose the "For You" album.
- Select All to see all of your past experiences. Alternatively, you may press a memory to begin playing it, and then tap it again to access other features, such as Memory mixes and Browse. When you choose the Browse option, the music will keep playing and a gallery of all the stored images will appear.
- Automatically recommended memories will play indefinitely until you change the recommendation, replay, like, or share the currently playing memory.

Flip the Memory playlist.

Using a memory mix, you may apply a customized visual style and musical accompaniment to a certain experience. There are a number of pre-made "Memory mixes" available for each memory, or you may use Apple Music to create your own custom mix. How? Read on!

- Launch the Photo app and choose the "For You" tab.
- Select a past experience with a tap.
- To listen to various mixes, touch the screen, press the Memory mixes button, and then swipe left.
- Repeatedly touching the screen will apply the Memory blend.

Alter the way you remember

- Launch the Photo app and choose the "For You" tab.
- Select a past experience with a tap.
- Touch the display, then choose Memory mixes, and finally select Filters.
- Choose a look from the available Memory Looks, and then press the Done button.

Swap out the tunes in your head

If you're using iOS 15 or iPadOS 15, you may customize the background music for your saved photos and videos by selecting a new track or playlist. If you're an Apple Music user, you can also check out personalized song recommendations based on your tastes and the music that was playing when the memory was created. The tune may be altered as follows:

- Launch Camera Roll and choose the "For You" album.
- Select a past experience with a tap.
- Select a mix from your memory by first tapping the Music button.
- Tap Done when you've either found the desired tune in the list or performed a search for it.

Make your own recollections

To make your own Memories based on a selected album or calendar date:

- Select the album by clicking on the Albums menu item. You may also choose Months or Days from the Library menu.
- Select Play Memory Movie from the More menu.

While the movie is playing, touch the screen and choose More from the menu that appears.

- Select Add to Favorites.
- Select the Close button.
- ➢ To create a new Memory for a person in your People album:
- Select People from the Albums menu.
- Select the person's thumbnail, then click the More option.
- Choose to Make a Photo Album.

Document the experiences that mean the most to you.

- Select a fond recollection by clicking the For You menu item.
- Select More, and then Favorites to add an item.

On the For You tab, choose See All next to Memories, and then select Favorites to see your most treasured recollections. Simply hit the Favorite button one more to remove a memory from your saved list.

Reminisce on the good times.

To access the movie's editing and sharing features, play the movie from Memory and touch the screen.

Choose how you'd like to share by tapping the Share button.

The song of a shared memory travels with you wherever you go. If a music isn't compatible with the memory, you'll be given the option to choose another song.

Memories may be edited

You have some leeway in editing your Memories to make them more unique. The length of a memory may be adjusted in response to the amount of photographs it contains, and you can modify the title as well.

Title Rewrite

Access the recollection by selecting More.

- Select Save after editing the title.
- Edit a memory's picture album as needed.
- Relive a moment by pressing the screen.
- Simply choose Manage Photos after clicking the More option.
- Select the photographs you want to save and uncheck those you don't want.
- Choose the Done option.

How to Make a Favorite Picture a Memorable One

If you want to pause the playback, you may do so at any time.

- To create a key photo, first choose More, then Make Key Photo.
- To block a certain image from recall:
- If you want to pause the playback, you may do so at any time.
- Select More, then choose Forget About It from the menu.

Memory spans may be altered.

- Relive a moment by pressing the screen.
- Select "More," then "Short," "Medium," or "Long" to refine your search.

Depending on how many images are currently stored, you may only be presented with the Short and Medium duration choices.

HOW TO USE PHOTO ALBUM IN PHOTOS ON IPHONE

To browse and arrange your media files, create albums in the Photos app. Select Albums to browse your media collections sorted into subfolders such as Videos, Portraits, and Slow Motion. Additionally, you may view your pictures by where they were taken (in the Places album) or by who was in them (in the People album).

Both your whole picture collection in the order in which you contributed them, and your favorite images and videos, may be seen in the Recents and Favorites albums, respectively.

After clicking the Albums button at the screen's bottom, a list of albums appears under the My Albums and Shared Albums titles. There's a See All link right next to the My Albums section. The Add button may be found in the upper left area of the interface.

Albums created using iCloud Photos will be kept on the cloud. They are always up to date and available on any of your signed-in Apple devices. See View photos from your iPhone in iCloud.

Make a recording album.

- Select Albums from the drop-down menu.
- Select New Album by tapping the Add button.

This is the Albums tab. A new album, folder, or shared album may be created by clicking the New Album button in the upper left corner.

- Album naming is followed by a Save button.
- To add media to the album, touch the thumbnails of the media you wish to include.

Insert a media file into an existing album.

- Select Library, double-tap an image or video to make it full screen, and then select More Options.
- Select "Add to Album," then select one of the following options:
  o Create a new recording: Select New Album, and then rename the album.
  o Put in a preexisting album: Choose an album you've already created by clicking My Albums.

Create an album with several media files.

- Choose All Photos or Days from the Library menu.
- Select will appear at the top of the screen; from there, you may press the thumbnails of the photos and videos you wish to upload before tapping the More Options option.
- Select "Add to Album," then select one of the following options:
  o Create a new recording: Select New Album, and then rename the album.

o Put in a preexisting album: Select an already album from the My Albums menu.

Album renaming

In Photos, an album's name may be changed at any time.

- To rename an album, go to Albums and then press it.
- Select Album, then Rename from the menu that appears.
- Just type in the new name and hit the save button.

HOW TO EDIT, SHARE AND ORGANIZE ALBUMS IN IPHONE

Albums in the Photos app may be edited, renamed, rearranged, and even deleted. Multiple albums may be stored in a single folder. Make a folder labeled "Vacations," for instance, and use it to store individual photo albums documenting each trip. Folders inside folders are also an option.

Compile a collection of images

- Launch the iPhone's photo album.
- Go to Albums, then double-tap the album you want to listen to.

- Select "More" from the menu bar, or "Add" from the gallery's bottom row of images.
- Select the photographs or videos you want to add to the album, and then tap Add photographs.

If you're looking for pictures from a certain era or location, try typing those terms into the search bar at the top of the page.

- Select Plus.

Take pictures out of a scrapbook

- Launch the iPhone's photo album.
- To delete a picture or video, go to the Albums tab, choose the appropriate album, and then press the item you want to delete.
- Select an option by tapping the trash can icon:
- When you choose "Remove from Album," the image disappears from that specific album but continues to exist in your collection and other albums.
- When you choose "Delete from Library," the image disappears from your library and all of your albums, and it is instead placed in the Recently Deleted folder.

- Select, then press the thumbnails of the photographs and videos you wish to delete, and last, hit the Trash Can icon to delete them all at once from the album.

Modify a picture album's layout and presentation.

Photos in an album may be seen in various sizes and aspect ratios.

- Launch the iPhone's photo album.
- Go to Albums, then double-tap the album you want to listen to.
- Select "More," and then choose an option:
- o Focus in
- o Panning Out
- o Image Resolution Grid

Publish a collection of pictures

You may choose which images from an album to share, or you can share the whole album.

- Launch the iPhone's photo album.
- Go to Albums, then double-tap the album you want to listen to.
- Select the media files you want to send out by tapping on them.

- Quickly and easily share all of the media included in an album by using the Select All button.
- Select a sharing method (AirDrop, Messages, Mail, etc.) by tapping the Share button, and then transmit the item.

Sort music and get rid of old records

- Launch the iPhone's photo album.
- Select Albums, then click on View All.
- Select Modify and make the required changes:
- You can rearrange things by touching and holding the album's thumbnail, and then dragging it to a new spot.
- The Delete button is used to delete.
- Choose the Done option.

Albums like Recents, People, and Places that Photos generate for you cannot be removed.

Create folders to store photo albums

- Launch the iPhone's photo album.
- Select Albums and then the plus sign to add.
- Select New Folder.
- Give the file a name, and then hit Save.

To make a new album or subfolder within the folder, open it, go to Edit, and then click the Add button.

CHAPTER TEN

HOW TO SET WHITE BALANCE ON IPHONE

With the introduction of iOS 17, the white balance may be locked in the Camera app for more precise control over your video recordings. The white balance setting of a camera controls what hue "white" really is. As a consequence, a standard is established against which variations in hue may be judged. This aids in correcting white, which may not always seem "white" depending on the lighting. When the white balance is locked, the camera will not automatically adjust the colors captured of the subject when the situation or illumination changes. If you're shooting a video with your iPhone and using iOS 17, you may lock the white balance so that it doesn't change while you shoot.

iOS 17 and Later Allows You to Lock White Balance on Your iPhone's Camera

First things first, let's define white balance and see why it's so important to maintain it.

The meaning of "White Balance"

The phrase "white balance" refers to the adjustments made to a picture or digital image to ensure that whites are rendered accurately regardless of the lighting conditions during capture. It's important because the color temperature of the light coming from different sources may alter how colors seem in real life.

The "white balance" option on your camera ensures that whites are really white in your footage and stills. It ensures that the colors in your films and photos are true to life by getting rid of any false color casts.

Regardless of the lighting circumstances, your captured footage or stills will seem more natural and professional if the white balance has been properly adjusted.

The iPhone's White Balance — What Is It?

The white balance setting on an iPhone camera defines the process of changing the colors in recorded footage so that white objects seem to be neutral and true colors regardless of the lighting conditions. Your iPhone's camera has an automated white balancing function that adjusts the camera's exposure in order to capture natural colors regardless of the illumination.

The automatic white balance function analyzes the surrounding light and adjusts the color temperature and tint settings accordingly to provide natural looking hues. The video's whites will seem pure white without any color tint from the lighting.

It is possible for an iPhone camera app to include both automated and manual white balance adjustments. These knobs allow for manual modification of the White Balance settings, allowing you to achieve a specific color temperature or compensate for challenging lighting conditions.

When shooting in manual white balance, most cameras will let you to choose from a number of different lighting conditions, such as daylight, cloudy, fluorescent, and tungsten. You may use a white or neutral-gray object as a reference when setting the white balance, which is an option provided by several camera programs.

Capturing films with correct and natural color with your iPhone's white balancing function is possible in a variety of lighting circumstances. It allows you to make sure your films have the most accurate colors possible, which results in more stable and pleasant visuals.

How does iPhone's White Balance Lock work?

You can prevent the white balance from shifting whenever you move the iPhone camera by using the white balance lock option. Once you've settled on a certain white balance setting, your camera will remember it even if you replicate a picture or the lighting changes.

The camera's white balance is often pre-set and dynamically altered in response to the surrounding light. However, there are instances when keeping the white balance consistent across several images or settings is desirable.

If you use the "White Balance Lock" function, your camera won't alter your white balance setting, no matter how the illumination changes. Particularly helpful for preserving color and atmosphere in films shot in locations with a variety of light sources.

When shooting in challenging lighting or with many exposures, locking the white balance gives you finer control over the overall color temperature and hue of your photos.

Method for Instantly Fixing iPhone Camera's White Balance

- Make sure iOS 17 is installed on your iPhone first.
- Launch the iPhone's Settings application to get started.
- Select Camera's Open Settings by scrolling down and tapping on Camera.
- Select Record video thereafter.
- Finally, activate Lock White Balance by toggling its switch on.
- Then, after selecting Lock White Balance, tap the Record button.

Congratulations, you have just finished setting the white balance on your iPhone's camera. Now you may start recording movies in the Camera app without having to constantly adjust the white balance.

IF THE CAMERA OR FLASH ON YOUR IPHONE IS NOT WORKING

Here's what to do if your camera's screen goes dark or your pictures come out fuzzy.

Take everything apart and put it through its paces.

Take off any film, case, or accessory that might prevent the camera's flash from firing or that could attract a magnet to the device.

See how well the camera works by taking a picture.

A quick test of the LED light:

If you have an iPhone or iPad, you can use the built-in flashlight in Control Center. If you're using an iPad or iPhone model X or later, slide down from the top right corner of the display. Swipe up from the bottom of the screen on an iPhone 8 or before.

- Select the Flashlight Icon with a tap.

If your device's flash is inconsistent, launch the Camera app and choose a new setting by tapping the flash button.

The camera may be turned off via a Mobile Device Management (MDM) profile or another configuration profile.

Additional stages may be tried independently if desired.

If the camera still isn't functioning, you may attempt these additional troubleshooting steps on your own if you choose. Even if you follow all of these instructions to the letter, you may still need to call Apple Support.

If the picture is fuzzy, try wiping the lenses with a microfiber cloth. Contact Apple Support if you see any dirt or debris within the lens, any damage to your iPhone around the camera, or if the camera lens seems misaligned or obstructed.

If you utilize a lens converter, metallic case, or magnetic lens attachment and are experiencing motion blur in low light, uninstalling the accessory may help.

Turn off and back on your Apple device again.

Put the most recent version of iOS on your iPhone.

Take another snap to see whether the camera is working. You should check to see whether either the front or back camera is malfunctioning. You may alter perspectives by using the rotate button.

MAKE YOUR IPHONE YOUR OWN

The iPhone may be personalized to suit the user's own tastes. Modify the font size, modify the ringtone, and vibration settings for incoming calls and texts, as well as other functions.

The iPhone's command hub.

Easily access your most used functions.

The iPhone's flashlight, timer, and calculator are all accessible with a single swipe from Control Center. Swipe down from the top right corner of the screen on an iPhone equipped with Face ID to access Control Center; swipe up from the bottom of the screen on an iPhone equipped with a Home button to do the same.

- In Settings, tap Control Center to add tools like a magnifier and alarm clock.

The iPhone's Lock Screen may be personalized with the help of the Add New Wallpaper screen, which displays a gallery of wallpaper options.

Change the Lock Screen Picture

You may customize the time and date as well as the typeface of a featured picture and widgets.

Start by touching and holding the Lock Screen, and then selecting Add New from the options that appear. Look through the gallery, and then choose one to edit its look. When you've made a custom Lock Screen you like, choose it by tapping Add and then selecting Set as Wallpaper Pair.

The iPhone's Home Screen includes the Weather, Reminders, and Home widgets. The Home and

Reminders widgets both include interactive elements.

Organize your Home Screen using widgets.

Using widgets, you may quickly access the data that matters to you most, such as the weather and your schedule. You can also accomplish things, like playing a song from your Music library or crossing something off your to-do list in Reminders.

When the applications on a Home Screen page jitter when you touch and hold the page's backdrop, you're ready to add a widget.

The iPhone's call screen, customized with a personal Contact Poster.

Calls may be personalized.

Make a customized call poster so that people always know who is calling them. Select an image or emoji, match it with the typeface and color scheme of your choice. The person you are contacting might see your call poster when you make a phone call.

- To begin, launch Contacts, touch your name, and then choose Contact Photo & Poster.

The Controls menu option for Sound and Touch. Headphone Audio and Headphone Safety are at the top of the screen, followed by a volume slider and buttons to modify the loudness of ringtones and alerts, and finally Sounds and Haptic Patterns, where you can customize things like the ringtone and the text tone.

Pick out some sensations and noises

The iPhone may play ringtones, vibrate, or display alerts for incoming calls, texts, and calendar events.

- Navigate to the Menu > Preferences > Sound and Touch. In the Contacts app, you may customize the ringtones and text tones that are played for individual contacts by tapping the name of the contact, selecting Edit, and then selecting the appropriate option.

The following in-built functions may be seen in order from top to bottom on the Accessibility screen inside Settings: Physical and motor features, such as Touch ID, Face ID, and Attention, and sensory features, such as VoiceOver, Zoom, Display and Text Size, Motion, Spoken Content, and Audio Descriptions.

Take use of in-built accessibility tools

The iPhone has various features that cater to those with visual, motor, auditory, and cognitive disabilities. Adjust the font size, simplify the usage of the touchscreen, and use your voice to operate your iPhone.

- Go to "Settings" > "Accessibility" to make changes to these options.

This is the Sharing and Access Management page for Safety Check under the Preferences menu.

Verify your security settings

The iPhone is built with security and privacy in mind. You have the option to allow applications to follow your activities across the apps and websites of other firms, or to disable this feature altogether. The Safety Check feature also allows you to manage which contacts and applications have access to your data. Navigate to Privacy & Security under Settings.

ADJUST A PHOTO'S LIGHT, EXPOSURE AND MORE IN PHOTOS ON MAC

The Photos app has simple controls for adjusting exposure and color. Photos can evaluate your image and automatically apply the optimal combination of edits to make your shot seem its best. Exposure, highlights, shadows, brightness, and contrast are just some of the settings that may be fine-tuned by revealing the granular controls. Also, video editing is supported.

A simple way to access the editing tools is to tap the letter A.

Perform simple edits on photographs

- To edit an image in Photos, double-click it and choose Edit from the menu bar.
- In the menu bar, choose Adjust.
- To adjust the photo's brightness, color, or black and white, choose the corresponding arrow and move the slider to the desired setting.
- Select "Auto" to have Photos do the fixing for you.

The Adjust panel's Light, Color, and Black & White sliders. Over the sliders is an Auto button.

As a helpful hint, you may undo your modifications to a certain slider by double-clicking it. A blue checkmark will display next to the name of the modification to show that it has been updated. To temporarily activate or deactivate the modification and see its impact on the image, just pick or deselect the checkbox.

Fine-tune the brightness.

178

A photo's lighting may be tweaked even further for optimal results.

- To edit an image in Photos, double-click it and choose Edit from the menu bar.
- In the toolbar, choose Adjust, then the arrow next to Light, and finally the arrow next to Options.
- To alter the style of the picture, just drag one of the sliders

Brightens shadows, brings out highlights, and boosts contrast to bring out latent information in a shot; therefore, the name "Brilliance." Although there is no actual change to the colors in the picture, the adjustment may make them seem different because of the increased contrast in the brighter areas.

The exposure setting allows the user to control the overall contrast of the picture.

- ✓ Modifies the level of highlighting.
- ✓ Changes how much depth is seen in shadows.
- ✓ Adjust the photo's brightness using the "Brightness" slider.
- ✓ Adjusts the level of contrast in the image.

The black point is the point at which the darkest areas of the picture lose all of its luminance and become utterly undefined. When the black point is adjusted, a washed-out picture gains contrast.

The range of a slider may be increased by positioning the cursor over it and pressing and holding the Option key.

Tweak the colors

Saturation, vibrancy, and color cast are all aspects of a picture that may be fine-tuned.

- To edit an image in Photos, double-click it and choose Edit from the menu bar.
- In the toolbar, choose Adjust, then the arrow next to Color, and finally the arrow next to Options.
- To alter the style of the picture, just drag one of the sliders:
- ➤ Saturation, Vibrance, and Cast sliders in the Color section of the Adjust panel.
- ➤ Saturation changes how strongly each color appears in the shot.

Adjusts the level of contrast between different colors and the degree to which they are separated in the image.

Cast: Modifies and corrects the photo's color cast.

The range of a slider may be increased by positioning the cursor over it and pressing and holding the Option key.

Adjust the grayscale details as needed.

A photo's grain may be adjusted, and its tonal and grayscale ranges can be tweaked.

- To edit an image in Photos, double-click it and choose Edit from the menu bar.
- Choose Black & White by clicking the arrow next it in the toolbar, then selecting Options by clicking the arrow beside it.
- To alter the style of the picture, just drag one of the sliders:

Intensity, Neutrals, Tone, and Grain sliders in the Black & White section of the Adjust window.

The intensity slider adjusts the brightness of the photo's tones.

Lightens or darkens the image's neutral tones.

- ✓ Tone: Makes the image brighter or darker, increasing or decreasing contrast.

✓ Grain: lets you modify the visible film grain in the image.

CHAPTER ELEVEN

TIPS AND TRICKS FOR IPHONE 15 CAMERA

Here are some of the finest ways to get started with your new iPhone 15 or iPhone 15 Plus:

1. Explore the Evolving Island

The notch on the iPhone 15 and iPhone 15 Plus has been replaced with a Dynamic Island, much like the iPhone 14 and the iPhone 13 before it. You can interact with the Dynamic Island, which means that the pill-shaped box will display applications and other iPhone functions.

What Dynamic Island may show by default includes:

- ✓ Verifications of Apple Pay purchases
- ✓ Discretion alerts for the usage of a microphone or camera
- ✓ Sending data through AirDrop
- ✓ the health of the AirPods' connection and its battery
- ✓ Battery health and charge levels on an iPhone
- ✓ Battery warnings

- ✓ The option to toggle silence
- ✓ Face recognition unlocking
- ✓ Unlocking using an Apple Watch
- ✓ Using Near Field Communication
- ✓ Connections through AirPlay
- ✓ The shift in focus mode
- ✓ Abbreviated procedures
- ✓ No-data/flight-mode notifications
- ✓ Notifications sent to your SIM card
- ✓ Connecting Parts and Pieces
- ✓ Discover the Notifications I've Set Up
- ✓ Shortcuts
- ✓ Maps with upcoming stops and routes
- ✓ Caller ID and time spent on the line
- ✓ Song duration remaining
- ✓ Automatic timers
- ✓ Current Status Updates
- ✓ Collaborative games
- ✓ Taking a Screencast
- ✓ Take notes verbally
- ✓ Hotspot access for one's own use

Apps that are compatible with the Dynamic Island may be installed, and any data from a Live Activity will show up there. You can monitor automobile trips, watch games, and check times.

2. Enable Face ID for Secure Safari Browsing

Safari's Private Browsing mode lets you navigate the web without logging any of your activity (cookies, history, etc.). But if you use Private Browsing and have tabs open, those tabs will remain even after you end your session. Instead, they remain open in Safari until you dismiss them, making it possible for anybody who gains access to your phone to see your private browsing history.

This new feature in Safari's Private Browsing mode, introduced with iOS 15, allows you to restrict access to it. To utilize this feature, you must first turn it on.

The option to need Face ID to unlock private browsing may be found in Safari's settings. That's all, you're all set! To try it out, use Safari and go to Preferences > Security > Private Browsing. If you try to switch to private browsing, you'll need to utilize Face ID to get into your secret windows.

3. Remove verification codes from your account mechanically.

Two-factor authentication, or 2FA, requires a verification code to be delivered to your phone or inbox before allowing access to a service. There's a new secret feature in iOS 15 that makes it simpler to clean up after accidentally receiving hundreds of verification codes in your text messages or email. Additionally, you'll need to manually activate it since it's disabled by default.

To enable automatic password cleanup, choose Passwords > Password Options in the Settings app. If you use the verification code using the autofill option at the top of your keyboard, all authentication alerts you get in Messages (or even in Mail) will be removed immediately. The verification code will remain in your messages or emails if you do not activate the autofill option.

4. With the new Camera Level feature in iOS 17, you can get your shots nice and level.

This iPhone 15 hack can let you create more professionally composed shots. You can now take use of a new, if rather buried, feature in your iPhone's built-in Camera app: a virtual horizontal level that appears while you take pictures. If you have the Level setting enabled and your iPhone detects that you are lining up a straight-on photo when the device is tilted slightly off of horizontal, a broken horizontal line will appear on the screen. When your phone is tilted at an angle, the line will be white; when it is properly oriented, it will change yellow.

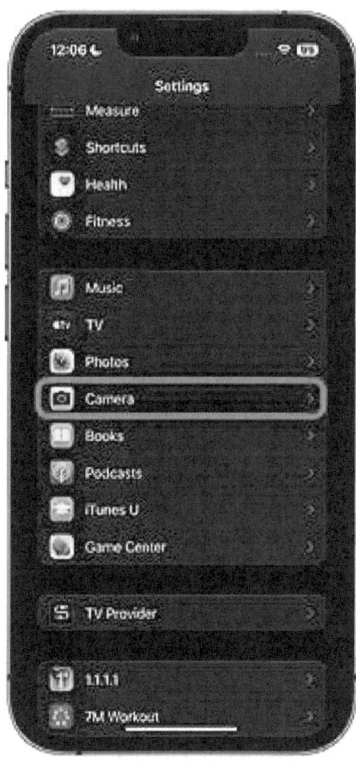

Again, this function is disabled by default and must be activated in the manner described below.

Initiate a visit to your iPhone's Settings menu.

Choose Camera after some scrolling.

In the "Composition" menu, activate the Level slider.

You should now be able to see the broken horizontal lines in the middle of the viewfinder whenever you launch the Camera app and attempt to take a subject at a right angle. Raise your angle so that the lines meet in a straight yellow line.

5. Use Apple Maps even when you're not connected.

One of the new features of the iPhone 15 is the ability to download Apple Maps and use it offline. If you know how to use Google Maps without an active internet connection, you'll be able to continue your journey even if you're in an area without access to Wi-Fi or cellular data.

To access Offline Maps in Maps, choose your profile picture from the menu bar's upper right corner. You may be presented with a recommended map to download based on where you often go, along with the map's file size in case you're low on space. Simply choose Download New Map, enter the name of a city, and make any necessary adjustments to the map before saving it to your iPhone.

6. Photos' zoom function is perfect for precise cropping.

Before iOS 16, you had to go through a few steps to crop a picture in the Photos app: tap into the Edit interface, choose the crop tool, and then use pinch zoom motions or drag the corners of the crop tool to make adjustments.

Thanks to iOS 17's simplifications, a new Crop button displays in the top-right corner of the screen whenever you zoom into a chosen picture in your photo library.

With only a touch, you may quickly and easily crop into the preferred area of the picture, rotate the image, reverse it, apply a screen ratio, or other Markup tools, all while maintaining the magnification level you've chosen. When you're through making your adjustments, press the Done button to save your cropped picture. However, you need to be fast since the crop option only displays for a short time after you zoom in on a picture.

7. To decipher washing machine codes, use a visual reference.

Do you know the meaning of the symbols on your laundry tags? You won't have to anymore thanks to a new feature in iOS 15 called Visual Lookup, which allows you to just take a photo of anything and instantly get relevant data.

Taking a clear picture of your laundry symbols, opening the **Photos **app, locating the image of the laundry symbols, swiping up, and tapping on Look Up Laundry Care are all that's required. The outcomes will reveal the significance of all laundry-related icons.

8. Smooth out the breaks in your music using Crossfade.

If you're like me, there are times when you don't want silence to interrupt the flow of an energizing playlist or leave you guessing about what's to come. There will be no more abrupt transitions between songs on your iPhone 15 thanks to a new feature.

Crossfade may be activated in the Music section of the Settings menu. Once this option is activated, the duration of the cross-fade may be adjusted from 1 to 12 seconds in 1 second increments. If you set the timer for five seconds, for instance, the next track from the album or playlist will begin playing softly in the background five seconds before the current song finishes.

9. Use your home screen widgets to do things

Widgets have been available on the home screen and lock screen of the iPhone since iOS 5.0. Now, with iOS 17, you can control playback, check off to-dos, and manage smart hone devices directly from the widgets themselves, without having to open any other apps.

To review, widgets make it possible to see data without opening a separate program. To-dos you have coming up, for instance, may be shown in a reminders widget for easy visual recall. On the other hand, widgets have traditionally remained unchanging; in order to complete the tasks listed in the Reminders widget, for example, you would have to open the app itself. That's not very handy, to put it mildly.

For certain widgets, iOS 17 brings interactivity. Widgets for the Reminders and Home applications are the first to get the new Interactivity functionality. Widgets are a convenient way to manage media playing in applications that have this capability, such as Music, Podcasts, Books, and News. The Safari widget provides quick access to articles in your reading list, while the Contacts widget expands on a selected contact's details (such as location, messages, and shared photographs) when tapped on. To add a widget to your home screen, long-press an empty area of your screen to enter edit mode, then touch the + symbol in the upper right.

10. Adjust Siri's Playback Volume and Speech Rate

With iOS 17, you may modify Siri's volume, timbre, and speaking rate on the iPhone 15.

When using Siri on the new iPhone 15, you may adjust the volume by activating the assistant and then saying "Speak louder" or "Speak quieter."

Follow these instructions to modify Siri's speech rate on the iPhone 15:

Accessibility may be accessed via the Settings menu.

Use the Siri button.

The Speaking Rate slider may be used to the right to increase the rate of speaking or to the left to decrease it.

11.   Go into Standby Mode

In iOS 17, Apple included a new Lock Screen option called StandBy, which appears whenever an iPhone is charging on its side. Imagine it as a smart display for your iPhone that provides instant access to several displays with glanceable information that can be read from a distance, such as while your phone is charging in the kitchen, on a desk, or in bed.

You must have the screen locked on your iPhone 15 and be charging phone in landscape orientation on a vertical charger for this mode to operate.

By default, the iPhone StandBy function will be active and appear automatically.

The default StandBy view combines a traditional analog clock and calendar widget on the right; to switch between them, just swipe up on either. Widgets may be added or removed by pressing and holding either button.

Swipe heavily from right to left on the first StandBy display to cycle through the available options.

To alter the appearance of the other StandBy views, just press and hold on them.

Settings > StandBy is where you'll find the options for adjusting standby.

12.   Make a Sign with Your Contact Information

You may personalize your image while calling someone by creating a contact poster. Contact Posters, which display on an iPhone user's screen when they get a call from you, may be customized with photographs and emoticons. Similarly to the iPhone Lock Screen, you may pair photos with striking text.

However, the Contact Poster isn't merely a calling feature. It's integrated into your contact card in the Contacts app as well, making it uniform across all of your platforms. The following procedures illustrate this process:

Access your own name in the Contacts list.

Select the Contact Poster & Image choice.

Customization may be achieved by selecting Edit followed by Customize.

Use the Poster.

Take a picture, choose one from your gallery, use a Memoji, or personalize it with only your initials using the buttons at the bottom of the screen.

You have the option of changing the font, size, and color to complement the picture you've uploaded. (It's important to note that this interface does not allow you to modify your display name; instead, you must edit your profile's contact information.)

Black and white, duotone, and a color wash of your choosing may all be previewed by swiping over the poster.

When you're satisfied with your call preview, press the Done button. If the appearance suits your tastes, choose Next.

You may now decide whether to trim your Contact Photo, choose a new photo, or skip this step altogether.

13.   Stop reading and start listening to the news!

If you like podcasts, you'll love this secret feature of the new iPhone 15: you can have Siri read aloud any item from a news site, any page from an educational website, or anything else you're seeing in Safari.

Choose an article and then click it in Safari. Articles bookmarked in your Reading List are also available for selection.

Take into account that at the present time, the iPhone 15 trick can only be used in Safari. Siri won't be able to read aloud anything that you've opened in a different browser or in a social network app like Twitter.

Simply speaking "Siri, read this to me" or "Hey Siri, read this to me" will invoke Apple's virtual assistant; the wake word "Hey" is no longer necessary as of iOS 17.

After then, Siri will start reading the piece out loud. Using the on-screen controller, you can play, stop, fast-forward, rewind, and access the AirPlay settings. The phrase "Siri, resume reading" will resume playing from the point you paused it.

Here's yet more approach to getting Siri to chat:

open up a story in Safari. Choose the AA symbol that appears in the address bar. Select Listen to Page from the option that appears.

Even though there are no obvious playback controls, Siri will begin reading to you. You may pause playback by tapping the Aa symbol again. The option will read Resume Listening if you have previously halted playing.

14.   Create a plethora of timers

Yes, for the first time, you may schedule several timers on an iPhone to begin at the same instant. This feature of the iPhone 15 comes in handy when you need to set separate timers for different parts of a recipe, such as when you're cooking. In iOS 17, users now have the ability to establish numerous timers and name them as needed.

Start by opening the Clock app, going to the timers tab, creating a new timer (giving it a name if you want), and then tapping Start. While it's still active, touch the + sign again to start again. And you'll have many timers working in parallel.

15.   Real-time voicemail

This new feature in iOS 15 is perfect for those who prefer to text instead of make phone calls. With Live Voicemail, you can see who is calling and decide whether you want to pick up without having to return their call.

When you first set up your new iPhone 15 Pro, the Live Voicemail function is activated.

The phone and recording symbol appears in the Dynamic Island or at the top of your iPhone whenever you get a call and choose to ignore it or send it to voicemail.

Select the phone icon to see the instant transcript of your Live Voicemail.

You may now ignore the caller, pick up the phone, or let them leave a message, and you can access Live message at any moment by swiping up from the bottom of the screen.

16.   Set your white balance

The option to lock the camera's white balance is another fantastic new feature in iOS 15. If you don't have this option selected, your camera may adjust the white balance of your movie mid-recording, causing a shift in the overall color temperature of the clip. It's possible that there are situations in which having your phone automatically adjust the white balance is preferable, such as when transitioning from natural to tungsten light. The answer is to lock white balance, which prevents your iPhone from changing white balance throughout the same clip.

The option to lock the white balance setting may be found by going to the camera's settings, then to Record Video, and then to the Settings menu.

Made in United States
Troutdale, OR
09/29/2024

23225096R00116